THE EDUCATION OF HEARING-HANDICAPPED CHILDREN

The education of
hearing-handicapped children

THOMAS J. WATSON, M.A., PH.D.

Reader in Audiology and Education of the Deaf
University of Manchester

UNIVERSITY OF LONDON PRESS LTD

SBN 340 06466 8

Copyright © 1967 Thomas J. Watson
Second impression 1969
All rights reserved. No part of this publication may be
reproduced or transmitted in any form or by any means,
electronic or mechanical, including photocopy, recording
or any information storage and retrieval system, without
permission in writing from the publisher.

University of London Press Ltd
St Paul's House, Warwick Lane, London EC4
Printed in Great Britain by
T. and A. Constable Ltd, Edinburgh

HV
2437
.W3
1967

Contents

ALMA COLLEGE
MONTEITH LIBRARY
ALMA, MICHIGAN

Introduction

The aim of this work is to present, in a relatively concise form, a broad picture of the principles involved in the provision of education for hearing-handicapped children. In the first section of the book an outline of the existing provision in Great Britain for these children is given together with brief comparative accounts of provision in some other countries. This section also deals with the tests used to discover deafness in childhood and the principles upon which educational placement should be based. The second section describes the education of deaf and partially hearing children, the use of hearing aids and the help that parents can give to their children whilst they are at school.

It is believed that this work fills a gap in the contributions that have been made in recent years to the field of the education of deaf children. It should be of particular value to those training to become teachers of the deaf, and it is hoped that teachers, parents and those responsible for the testing and placement of children with impaired hearing will find it helpful.

SECTION ONE

PROVISION AND PLACEMENT

I

Present
educational provision
in Britain

The present provision of education for hearing-handicapped children in Great Britain is based on the English Education Act of 1944, the corresponding Scottish and Irish Acts of 1945 and 1947 and subsequent regulations. These Statutory regulations relate to two categories of pupils with defective hearing—those described as deaf and those described as partially deaf. In order to provide an omnibus term to cover the whole range of pupils with defective hearing the phrase 'hearing-handicapped' will be used in the present work wherever the whole group is being referred to. The use of such a term would seem to be consistent with the nomenclature used for groups of children with other types of handicap, viz., visually handicapped, mentally handicapped, physically handicapped and so forth.

The British Education Acts of 1944-47 were not the first measures of their kind to deal with the education of hearing-handicapped children, but in so far as they, and the subsequent regulations, have initiated a period which has seen a whole range of new developments in education as well as what seems to be a new philosophy of the education of hearing-handicapped children, they provide a convenient starting-point for the present chapter. At the same time it must not be forgotten that these Acts and Regulations built upon the existing pattern of schools whose educational methods had evolved over a period of one hundred and fifty years. It is not intended to describe the historical development of education for deaf children here, but it is important to recognise that some present trends have their origin in the nineteenth century and likewise that some current practices and arrangements are a continuation, in a contemporary setting, of what was done a hundred years ago.

The Education Act of 1944 laid down (cl. 33) that the Minister would make "regulations defining the several categories of pupils requiring special educational treatment and make provisions as to the special methods appropriate for the education of pupils in each category". Similar powers were given to the Secretary of State for Scotland and the Minister of Education for Northern Ireland. In 1945 the Handicapped Pupils and School Health Service Regulations were published to implement this clause. These Regulations were superseded by the School Health Service and Handicapped Pupils Regulations of 1953 which defined (amongst the categories of pupils requiring special educational treatment) two categories of hearing-handicapped pupils—deaf pupils and partially deaf pupils. Deaf pupils were defined as "pupils who have no hearing or whose hearing is so defective that they require education by methods used for deaf pupils without naturally acquired speech and language". Partially deaf pupils were defined as those "who have some naturally acquired speech and language but whose hearing is so defective that they require for their education special arrangements or facilities though not necessarily all the educational methods used for deaf pupils" (cl. 14). Further regulations published in 1959 and entitled The Handicapped Pupils and Special Schools Regulations did not amend this section of the 1953 Regulations.

The 1953 Regulations also stated that a blind or a deaf pupil should be educated in a special school "unless the Minister otherwise approves", and that partially deaf pupils (as well as those in other categories of handicap) should be educated in special schools or ordinary schools "as may be appropriate" (cl. 15). Clause 16 stated that the "special educational treatment to be provided for every handicapped pupil attending an ordinary school . . . shall be appropriate to his disability". In the 1959 Regulations these clauses relating to placement were revoked. It was, however, laid down that "the special educational treatment given in a school shall be efficient and suited to the age, ability and aptitude of the pupils, with particular regard to their disability of mind or body" (cl. 7). It was further ruled that "no pupil shall be admitted to a school or retained in it unless it is suitable for him having regard to his age and sex and to the nature of his handicap" (cl. 12). This, obviously, left the position much more flexible in determining placement. The Regulations also laid down that the maximum number of deaf and partially deaf children in a class was not to exceed ten.

Some anomalies in these regulations became apparent and the classification did not take into account the results of early ascertainment and home training. Earlier use of hearing aids sometimes resulted in children acquiring a considerable amount of spoken language before reaching the age at which attendance at school became compulsory. Were such children to be described as 'deaf' or 'partially deaf'? The description was important in view of the different placements available for each category. To remedy this situation Amending Regulations were passed in 1962 which redefined the two categories of hearing-handicapped pupils. Deaf pupils were described as those "with impaired hearing who require education by methods suitable for pupils with little or no naturally acquired speech or language". The other category was re-named 'partially hearing pupils', that it to say "pupils with impaired hearing whose development of speech and language, even if retarded, is following a normal pattern, and who require for their education special arrangements or facilities though not necessarily all the educational methods used for deaf pupils". Perhaps even more significant than those changes in the regulations was the accompanying circular (10/62) which pointed out that the intention of these changes was "to reflect a more positive approach to the use of residual hearing, and in this way to underline the importance of early diagnosis", that the regulations did not attempt to give more than a broad classification and that many factors needed to be taken into account in determining placement. These factors included stage of linguistic development, lipreading ability, auditory discrimination and character traits, as well as the possibility of complicating handicaps. It stressed the need for consultation and team-work in placement as well as the desirability of regular review.

The Act of 1944 had also laid down that local authorities had the duty of ascertaining what children in their areas required special educational treatment (cl. 34). Local authorities were authorised to examine children from the age of two years for this purpose. Parents could also demand such an examination if they suspected the presence of a handicap. Special educational treatment could begin in nursery schools or classes from the age of two, although the lower age of compulsory attendance remained at five years, the same as for non-handicapped children. Attendance at a special school was still compulsory up to sixteen.

The Scottish and Irish Acts have not been discussed in detail, nor have the regulations outlining the form that special educational treatment should take been mentioned. Essentially these followed the pattern of the English Act and Regulations save that in Northern Ireland the Transfer of Functions (No. 2) Order, of 1948, made under the Public Health and Local Government (Administrative Provisions) Act of 1946 put the responsibility for the ascertainment and placement of handicapped (including deaf) pupils in the hands of the local health authorities. This meant that school medical officers were responsible to the health and not the education committees, with the result that a need for special educational treatment could be decided without consulting anyone connected with the education service. The dissatisfaction caused by this state of affairs resulted in sufficient pressure being brought to bear to have the order revoked.

There were, of course, when the Acts were passed a large number of schools administered by local authorities and voluntary committees. To a considerable extent the existing pattern of schools was in conformity with the proposals set out in the new legislation, but there were immediate deficiencies observable. Although there had been a separate school for partially deaf pupils in the west of Scotland from 1908 and rather lesser provision in the east of Scotland from 1936, there were no separate schools for partially deaf pupils in England. There had been some separate provision for such pupils in London County Council Schools from 1913 but this had gradually died out. Pupils who could be described as partially deaf were, if unable to profit from the education given in ordinary schools, to be found in schools for the deaf where they were formed into separate classes if numbers were sufficiently large for this to be done. In a pamphlet issued in 1946 (1) to explain and amplify the regulations it was pointed out that partially deaf pupils who needed full-time special educational treatment would require to attend either day schools for deaf and partially deaf pupils or a boarding school for the deaf which had a department for the partially deaf. It did, however, look forward to the possibility of establishing separate boarding schools for the partially deaf in future.

Accordingly, one voluntary body and a number of local education committees, acting upon this implied blessing, and recognising the need for such schools, opened boarding schools for partially deaf children. These, in chronological order, were the Liverpool School for the Partially Deaf at Birkdale, Lancashire, in 1948; Tewin Water School for the Partially Deaf, Hertfordshire, in 1953; and Needwood School for the Partially Deaf in Staffordshire in 1954. By arranging the transfer of its deaf pupils to Margate, the Brighton School for the Deaf was transformed into a school for the partially deaf in 1949.

In addition to the establishment of these boarding schools, special day classes for partially deaf children were re-established by the London County Council in 1947, in spite of an Advisory Council's suggestion (2) in 1938 that this kind of provision was not to be recommended. In fact, these units consisting of one or two classes attached to ordinary county primary schools proved to be highly successful and they have been added to by the London County Council and imitated by an increasing number of local authorities since.

Although the Advisory Committee referred to in the previous paragraph had in its report in 1938 advised that deaf and partially deaf pupils should be educated separately, it had not insisted on the need for the education to take place in separate schools. During the 1950s the Ministry of Education became increasingly aware that this was desirable and in 1956 it firmly declared its policy on this point. In the *Health of the School Child* for that year it was stated that "the policy of the Ministry of Education is that wherever practicable deaf and partially deaf children should not be educated together". Accordingly, during the past nine years, the Ministry has encouraged the enrolment of deaf and partially deaf children in separate schools and indeed has attempted to bring about the re-organisation of local provision to effect this principle. Some schools have been encouraged to admit only partially deaf pupils and wherever possible to transfer their deaf pupils to a school provided by another authority. A corresponding policy has been adopted with other authorities who have been asked to retain only deaf pupils and send their partially deaf children elsewhere. Such a policy, although both administratively and educationally convenient and appropriate, has raised considerable practical difficulties. Parents have been unwilling to have their children transferred from day to boarding schools when they happen to be of a different category from that catered for locally. Similarly, local authorities have been reluctant to meet the additional expenditure incurred when some pupils who would otherwise live at home and attend school on a daily basis have now to be maintained in the boarding school of another authority. It would seem that because of the relatively small numbers involved such a clear-cut division of categories is not practicable save in very large cities. On the other hand, the very considerable growth of classes of partially deaf pupils attached to ordinary primary and secondary schools points to the ready acceptance of this alternative as a way of meeting this separation of categories. Theoretically, this is probably a good solution, although again in the case of smaller authorities the numbers are so small as to make anything like a homogeneous class in terms of age, ability and needs virtually impossible. There is, moreover, a risk that because this is a relatively cheap way of educating a hearing-handicapped child some children whose educational needs cannot be fully met in this way will be sent to these classes.

The consequence of local authorities acting in accordance with these statutory requirements and utilising the pre-1964 structure of educational provision for hearing-handicapped children is that the arrangements listed below in Table 1 indicate approximately the extent of the present provision. The total number of pupils catered for in these different types of provision is given in Table 2.

In addition to the schools and classes which are controlled by local authorities or voluntary committees there are five independent schools in Britain with an enrolment, in January 1964, of 270 pupils of whom 187 are categorised as deaf and eighty-three as partially hearing.

The provision of primary education is taken by the Education Acts noted above to include educational provision for children between the ages of two and five years in nursery schools or classes. Although there had been provision for deaf children below the age of five years before the passing of the Acts this was meagre and sporadic. Emphasis on the need for an early beginning to education increased as a result of the writings of the Ewings in the 1940s and the establishment of pre-school clinics and parent guidance programmes at the University of Manchester and later at the Royal National Throat, Nose and Ear Hospital in London. Teachers and administrators recognised the significance of this early start to education and the number of children ready to enter a nursery programme was increased as a result of the earlier ascertainment in the clinics and the help that parents were being given. Circular 23/61, issued by the Ministry of

Table 1   Establishments of different types for hearing-handicapped pupils in Great Britain in January 1964

	Schools for the deaf and partially hearing	Schools for the partially hearing	Classes for the partially hearing attached to ordinary schools
England & Wales	46	4	117
Scotland	9	3	2
N. Ireland	1	0	8
Total	56	7	127

Table 2   Numbers of pupils in different types of establishments in January 1964

	Deaf pupils in schools for deaf and partially hearing	Partially hearing pupils in schools for deaf and partially hearing	Deaf and partially hearing pupils in other special schools	Pupils in classes for partially hearing
England & Wales	3,070	1,578	158	916
Scotland	456	330	—	18
N. Ireland	96	44	—	65
Total	3,622	1,952	158	999

Health in September 1961, emphasised again the importance of early diagnosis and suggested ways in which local authorities might improve their methods of case-finding. It encouraged the establishment of audiology clinics and stressed the very great importance of beginning auditory training before children had reached the age of five years.

These developments, therefore, have resulted in a greater demand on the part of parents for nursery education and a greater willingness on the part of authorities to supply it in view of their recognition of its value. A new nursery/infant school was opened

B

by the Berkshire authority in 1949 and many other schools began to provide separate nursery and infant departments. The result of these developments was that the number of pupils below the age of five receiving full-time special educational treatment rose rapidly from 1947 onwards, the rate of increase being greatest in the period 1947-52. Table 3 shows this development.

Table 3   Hearing-handicapped children under five years receiving full-time special educational treatment

	1947	1952	1957	1962
No. of pupils under 5 years of age	139	317	350	399
The above no. expressed as a percentage of total enrolment	3·9	6·7	7·0	8·3

The Education Acts laid a duty on local education authorities to provide secondary education for all their children. Whilst it was not required that primary and secondary education should be given separately in special schools there was nothing in the Acts to suggest that secondary education in some form should not be provided for hearing-handicapped pupils. Traditionally, schools for the deaf had been all-age schools but, generally speaking, the education provided for the older pupils was an extension of elementary education rather than a form of secondary education. This was, of course, partly due to the limitations imposed by the handicap, particularly in linguistic development. Backwardness in basic educational attainments resulting from this limitation, and accentuated by the delay in beginning schooling to five years or later, made true secondary education seem an impossible task to many teachers. The first change in the climate of opinion came with the recognition that at least the brighter children could benefit from a more advanced education than was being generally provided. This idea had been generated before the nineteenth century closed, but its translation into practice, except in cases of a few pupils in private schools, did not take place until after the passing of the Education Acts. The first secondary school for deaf pupils was the Mary Hare Grammar School, opened in 1946. From an enrolment in that year of forty-four (only fifteen of whom were true grammar school candidates) the school has grown to its present strength of 150 pupils. Entrance is by a selection procedure involving written and oral examinations and pupils from any school in the United Kingdom who are thought likely to benefit from a grammar school education may be entered for the selection examination. Pupils generally remain until they are eighteen or nineteen years of age and local authorities assume financial responsibility for their own children. Most pupils proceed to the examination for the General Certificate of Education at Ordinary Level and a number continue up to Advanced Level. The results of the 1964 examinations are given below in Table 4, as an example of what can be achieved.

Table 4   G.C.E. Results, 1964—Mary Hare Grammar School
There were fifty-three candidates altogether, of whom eight obtained the eighteen passes at 'A' Level.

Subject	Number of Passes	
	'A' Level	'O' Level
Art	1	12
Biology	4	14
Chemistry	7	13
Cookery	–	6
English Language	–	5
English Literature	1	4
Engineering Drawing	–	2
French	–	8
General Literature	–	9
General Science	–	16
Geography	–	10
Geology	–	2
History	1	14
Physics	1	2
Mathematics	3	11
Additional Mathematics	–	1
Needlework	–	5
Use of English	–	3

To provide for the secondary education of deaf boys whose abilities lay more in the direction of technical studies, a secondary school with a technical bias for deaf boys was opened at Burwood Park, Surrey, in 1955. This school caters for thirty-five boys and at present uses the same selection procedure as the Grammar School. In 1964 the examination successes at the school included twelve candidates who gained thirty-one passes in six subjects [Art, Geometrical Drawing, Mathematics A, Mathematics B, Physics and Science (Building and Engineering)] in G.C.E. at Ordinary Level and fourteen candidates who gained fifty-four passes in ten subjects in the Royal Society of Arts School Certificate Examination.

When, in 1949, the counties of Berkshire, Hampshire and Surrey decided to co-operate in the provision of educational services for their deaf children, it was not only agreed that the nursery school should be provided by Berkshire* but that Surrey should provide the secondary school. This school is situated in Nutfield Priory at Redhill and provides a secondary modern curriculum for eighty pupils from the three counties. The pupils are unselected and follow a five-year course with the possibility of choosing from a wide variety of subjects. The school has issued its own Leaving Certificate for passes in individual subjects and is now preparing to enter pupils for the Certificate of Secondary Education.

In order to meet the needs of pupils who were unable to secure entrance to the two selective secondary schools a number of all-age schools for the deaf and partially hearing have attempted to make some kind of provision for secondary education by arranging for pupils to attend technical and art courses held in schools and institutions for hearing pupils. Sometimes the pupils have continued to live in the school for the deaf and attend day classes elsewhere on either a full-time or a part-time basis; other schools have sent pupils to attend evening classes in various subjects. At the same time a few schools for the deaf and partially hearing have established secondary courses for selected pupils. Some details of the nature of these courses are given in Chapter 5, where there is also a discussion of future needs at this stage. One or two schools have even begun to provide courses leading to the G.C.E. examinations for a few pupils. Examples of this are St John's Institution at Boston Spa where, in 1962, seven pupils secured thirteen passes at Ordinary Level, and Needwood School for the Partially Hearing where, in the same year, four pupils obtained twelve passes at Ordinary Level.

These developments at the secondary stage are likely to be

* Now closed.

increased in the next few years and it is important that they should if the general academic level is to be raised and pupils fitted for more skilful and highly paid occupations.

The clause in the 1944 Act which proposed compulsory further education has not, as yet, become effective, but some attempts to provide this, mainly in the form of special evening classes, have been begun by teachers and institutes for the adult deaf, particularly in the north of England. In Glasgow, a day release class for deaf boys has been set up in one of the technical colleges, making use of an interpreter provided by the missioner to the adult deaf. Vocational training courses, on a full-time basis, are provided for deaf boys and girls between the ages of sixteen and eighteen at the Royal Residential Schools for the Deaf, Manchester. The trades taught are carpentry and baking (including catering and cake decoration) for the boys and cake decoration for the girls. The pupils seem to have no difficulty in obtaining suitable employment on completion of their courses.

The principle of educational provision as laid down in the Education Acts was that it should be suited to the different ages, abilities and aptitudes of the pupils. Accordingly, in the case of hearing-handicapped pupils who were dually- or multi-handicapped, the provisions described so far required to be supplemented. Cerebrally palsied, educationally subnormal, maladjusted, or delicate hearing-handicapped children cannot be appropriately educated in schools for pupils who have not these additional handicaps (unless they are minimal), either to their own benefit or to that of the other pupils. Provision for these additionally handicapped pupils is as yet inadequate and is mainly supplied by three or four schools and some smaller units. The Inner London Education Authority school at Rayners in Buckinghamshire provides for educationally subnormal and maladjusted pupils who are partially hearing. The school at Harewood, provided by the West Riding local education authority, admits a small number of educationally subnormal deaf and partially hearing boys. There is also a deaf/blind unit at the school for blind children with additional handicaps at Condover Hall, Shrewsbury. Three schools for cerebrally palsied children have small additional classes for those with the additional handicap of deafness, and the Belmont Hospital in Surrey provides facilities for mentally retarded deaf children.

In addition to the pupils so provided for it has been estimated that there are at least another 150 hearing-handicapped pupils who are being educated in schools for the deaf and partially hearing whose transfer to other schools would be most advantageous to themselves and to the other pupils in the schools.

So far, only the provision for hearing-handicapped pupils in special schools has been considered. It will be remembered, however, that the 1953 Regulations laid down that a partially deaf pupil might be educated "in a special school or an ordinary school as may be appropriate in his case" (cl. 15), and that the 1959 Regulations stressed that the education should be in accordance with his age, ability and aptitude. There are, in fact, a greater number of hearing-handicapped pupils who continue to be educated in ordinary schools than there are in special schools. The exact incidence of impaired hearing in those outside special schools is unknown and is likely to vary from area to area. In some areas, for example Cheshire, special investigations have been made to identify these children, and although a very considerable number has been found it is evident that not all such cases are as yet known to the authorities. In Cheshire, the number of children with significant hearing impairments in ordinary schools would indicate an incidence of about two per thousand although it is recognised that the information must be incomplete. It seems likely that there is a further ten per thousand with a considerable loss which in some cases could be an educational handicap. A wider survey, made of a total school population of about two and a half million children, suggested an incidence of 2·5 per thousand of the school population. It is also becoming clear that the incidence of defective hearing is likely to vary with different age groups. T. A. Clarke, reporting in 1961 (3), stated that 20 per cent of children in the six-year-old group suffered from otitis media in the period of a single year, whereas the overall incidence of cases found at school medical inspections was only 1·2 per cent. In a current survey the present writer is finding the incidence of hearing impairment in five-year-olds to be about 11 per cent, but only in approximately 4 per cent of thirteen-year-olds. The catarrhal conditions which give rise to the hearing loss may well in many cases be only temporary and improve with time or treatment, but some of the children have a loss which is an educational handicap, at least temporarily. So far, no provision has been made for this temporary loss, which may last for two or three years, if not longer, and which may well be the cause of some educational retardation in the early years of schooling.

However, even if these temporary conductive losses are omitted from consideration, the indications are that there are likely to be at least twice as many children with significant impairments in ordinary schools as there are being educated in special schools and classes for deaf and partially hearing children. At present, something like 0·6 per thousand of the total school population are wearing hearing aids in ordinary schools. It seems likely that this number will grow although it is by no means certain that all these children are rightly placed.

Whilst it is clearly recognised that there can be no comparison in terms of the severity of their handicap between these two main categories of hearing-handicapped children, the fact remains that this less handicapped group is very evidently educationally handicapped, is more numerous than has previously been thought and has had less consideration in the past than it has deserved. The provision of free hearing aids which was instituted by the National Health Act of 1948 has been of very great service to such children and probably about one-third of the pupils with significant hearing impairments in ordinary schools have been supplied with aids. On the other hand, this free provision of aids has tended to mask the real problems of these children through the too facile assumption that the provision of a hearing aid will solve a partially hearing child's problems. The use of a hearing aid is by no means a panacea for the educational difficulties of such children, and without skilled advice and training the benefit conferred will be minimal, if any. An increasing number of local authorities are providing the services of peripatetic teachers to assist in the education of hearing-handicapped children in their county primary and secondary schools. One of the earliest authorities to make this provision was Lancashire which, in 1948, appointed three peripatetic teachers. The importance of this work has only been slowly recognised and the increase in numbers of teachers thus employed has been correspondingly tardy. Since about 1956, however, the practice has gained in popularity and there has subsequently been a much more rapid increase in the number of appointments. At present, no fewer than thirty-six local education authorities employ one or more peripatetic teachers on their staffs with a total throughout England and Wales of ninety-four. It seems that many of these teachers give active help, on a weekly basis, to between twenty and thirty pupils and have a further seventy or eighty pupils for whom they are responsible in an advisory capacity. Their functions thus include advising pupils and teachers on the most effective ways of utilising the residual hearing of the former and giving regular help to more severely handicapped pupils in such matters as the use of hearing aids, speech improvement, and, occasionally, remedial teaching in the basic subjects.

Another method of dealing with the problems of these children is exemplified in the arrangement for a small group of boys, fully integrated into normal classes, to have a few periods each week with a qualified teacher of the deaf who is a member of the staff. The teacher of the deaf gives appropriate individual help to the hearing-handicapped boys for a varying number of periods each week, depending on individual needs, and, additionally, takes certain subjects with regular classes. A similar arrangement for pupils at the secondary stage was introduced by the London County Council in 1963. This pattern of provision, under the title of 'resource teacher', is found in the United States of America and its implications will be noted later.

It would be justifiable to conclude that during the post-war years a more flexible pattern of providing appropriate educational facilities for hearing-handicapped pupils has begun to emerge. To a greater or lesser extent all the elements in that pattern are now present so that the aim of the Education Acts to provide facilities appropriate to the age, ability and aptitude of the pupils is beginning to be realised, with the exception of the provision for further education. This does not mean that all the services are as yet complete. Clearly, it has not been possible to draft an ideal 'blueprint' and so many of the changes needed to implement the new philosophy had to be made within the existing arrangement of schools. This has meant that the process of change has had to be a gradual one. Moreover, although the elements of this new pattern are present, the lack of universality is in part the result of an uneven distribution of population throughout the country, making the provision of certain types of educational facility inappropriate or even virtually impossible in certain areas. It is also partly the result of the decentralisation of control over education. In Britain it appears to be the custom for the general policy to be worked out by the central government, but the actual means of implementing this policy is left to the local education authority. This may have weaknesses in some directions but it has strength in others, particularly in giving opportunities to local authorities to experiment with ideas and to make arrangements which they believe to be appropriate to their own local conditions. This flexibility is a powerful lever in promoting educational progress for, although the kind of education a pupil receives may be the fortuitous result of the area in which he was born, it is more conducive to the development of new and sound practical ideas than a rigid pattern imposed from above.

REFERENCES

1 *Special Educational Treatment* (1946). Ministry of Education Pamphlet No. 5. HMSO
2 *Report of the Committee of Enquiry into Problems Relating to Children with Defective Hearing* (1938). HMSO
3 Clarke, T. A. (1962). 'Deafness in Children'. *Proc. Royal Soc. of Med.* 55, 61

2

Educational provision made by some other countries

Some comparative studies on the provision of special education for children with defective hearing seem not to be out of place here since they serve to show how this problem is being met outside Great Britain and may suggest ways in which changes could be made in this country by taking advantage of experience elsewhere. An examination of the different ways in which this special education is provided will reveal the varying attitudes towards the place of deaf education within the educational framework of the country concerned and the aspirations for deaf children. The provision is, of course, related to a number of external factors such as economic, geographical and historical. Thus, when considering what is done in Norway and Sweden, this must be seen against a background of a comparatively large country with a small population, largely concentrated in one metropolitan area, where communications are difficult in certain parts. The incidence of defective hearing, at least so far as children requiring special educational help are concerned, is relatively small, so that density of population is a critical factor in determining the kind of provision that can be made. In a number of countries responsibility for provision does not rest with a Ministry of Education but with Ministries of Social Welfare or Public Health. This is partly a result of historical tradition but it tends to reflect an attitude to the education of deaf children which is different from that adopted in Great Britain or in other countries where the education of deaf children is an integral part of the educational pattern. When an educational system for unhandicapped children is not completely developed, as is the case in many emergent countries and in some European states where the national income is low, it is unlikely that special provision for handicapped children will be complete or even widespread.

As a consequence of all this, the adoption of a pattern which is successful in one country should not necessarily be recommended for use in another. Nevertheless, it remains true that much can be learned from what is being done elsewhere, and provided that the hazards of transplanting are fully realised it can be a fruitful exercise. With this in mind, the following brief accounts of the education of deaf and partially hearing children in a number of countries are given.

SCANDINAVIA

Denmark has a population of four and a half million. Of these, one and a quarter million live in the capital, Copenhagen. The country is mainly flat, agricultural land but is divided, like all Gaul, into three clear parts, each being separated from the other by a stretch of water. Communication, although not difficult, may not always be speedy and administratively each part (the islands of Funen and Zealand and the Jutland peninsula) tends to function in many ways as a separate entity.

Denmark was the first European country to make education compulsory for its deaf children. This was in 1817, ten years after the first school had been established in Copenhagen. Fifty years later, the deaf and hard of hearing were separated in different schools, each school having parallel classes for abler and less able children. This two-way division was the beginning of what became known as the Danish System which, with modifications, has persisted to the present day and provided a model for classification at least fifty years in advance of what most other countries were able to set up.

Present arrangements are based on the National Assistance Act of 1933 and the Education Act of 1950. A National Board for the Deaf was set up consisting of representatives of parents' councils, the state schools for the deaf and the Association of the Deaf. To this body local welfare boards, physicians and school principals have the duty of reporting all children in their area who have significant defects of hearing. All deaf children and most of the hard of hearing children over the age of seven years are examined at one of the three state centres (Copenhagen, Odense and Aarhus) which were established in 1950. Hearing aids are supplied there free, and hard of hearing children who are likely to be able to continue in ordinary schools are given help by local teachers who have received some training for this purpose at the centre and who are required to report periodically on progress. For hard of hearing children who require full-time special education there is a state school in Copenhagen which serves the city and north-eastern Zealand. Separate departments for these children are organised in the schools for the deaf at Fredericia and Aalborg. Classes for hard of hearing children are also attached to ordinary schools in Copenhagen, Aarhus and Esbjerg.

For severely and profoundly deaf children there is a state school at Copenhagen which also serves the eastern part of the country; state schools at Fredericia and Vejle for Funen and southern and central Jutland; and a school at Aalborg for the northern part of Jutland. In 1958 the number of pupils attending these schools and classes was:

State schools for the deaf	303
Schools for hard of hearing	200
Classes for hard of hearing	197
Attending ordinary schools with hearing aids	745

The state schools for the deaf, being 'special-care schools', are the responsibility of the Ministry for Social Affairs. Education is compulsory from the age of seven for a period of nine years, although it may begin sooner if the parents wish it. Since 1958 a continuation school has been established at Nyborg where a one-year course of further education is available to selected pupils on a voluntary basis. There is no formal vocational training in Denmark, but schools give pre-vocational training and vocational guidance.

In 1952 there was established in Copenhagen a State Examination and Guidance Clinic for Deaf and Hard of Hearing Children. There, pre-school children are tested audiologically and psychologically and guidance is given to the parents who follow a programme set up by the clinic in their own homes. They are visited regularly either by a worker from the clinic or by a teacher of the deaf from the school serving the district in which the child lives. During the summer vacation, workers from the clinic arrange a course for mothers with their deaf children at one of the state residential schools. There is also a kindergarten attached to the school for the deaf in Copenhagen but entry is generally confined to deaf children with additional handicaps.

Two features of the provision in Demark are worthy of special mention. The first is the boarding provision for children. Although few children outside Copenhagen and the larger towns are able to attend as day pupils, the Danes have contrived to avoid having large numbers of deaf children living together as a separate community. In many cases, particularly in Fredericia, Nyborg and Aalborg, foster homes are found for the children. Where this is not practicable, the pupils are accommodated in small groups of ten to twelve in separate houses.

The other feature is the establishment of an audiological laboratory in each of the state schools. They are well equipped, with an audiologist in charge who is responsible for measurement of hearing, recording speech and instructing staff in the use of a variety of aids to hearing.

It is also worthy of note that Denmark is one of the few European countries where a method of teaching other than purely oral is in use. This is the Mouth-Hand system, devised by Dr Forchammer, which involves manual symbols for the consonants in speech since many of these sounds are impossible either to lipread or distinguish. The symbols are made simultaneously with speech and the method is used at the junior stages. In point of fact many of the younger teachers seem to feel that the method is no longer in accordance with modern principles and accordingly make little, if any, use of it. This being so, it seems likely that it will fall into disuse within the next generation of teachers.

Norway with a population of only three and a half million has an area of between seven and eight times that of Denmark and is about one-third larger than the United Kingdom. With this low density goes considerable difficulty in communications owing to north-south mountain ranges and an extremely long, deeply indented coastline. Of this total population half a million live in the capital, Oslo. As a result of the scattered nature of the population all special schools in Norway are residential.

The first school for the deaf in Norway was established at Trondheim in 1825. Since 1881 education for deaf children has been compulsory between the ages of seven and sixteen years. The minimum period of attendance is eight years. The present organisation of schools results from the Law of 1951 which divided deaf and hard of hearing children into four categories or grades, almost identical with those proposed in the English

Report of the Committee on Children with Defective Hearing (1938). The educational provision is under the authority of the Ministry of Church and Education with a special branch known as the Directorate of Special Schools. All children who are deaf or severely hard of hearing must be reported by local councils and school boards to this directorate which makes arrangements for admission to the appropriate school. Education is free and the cost of board and maintenance is met by the local authority.

There are four state schools for the deaf: at Trondheim, Oslo, Holmestrand and Oyer. There is also a private school for mentally retarded deaf children at Andebu. On completion of the normal period of schooling there is provision for a two-year vocational training course. The vocational school for boys is in Bergen and prepares students mainly for the traditional trades of carpentry, shoe-repairing, tailoring and metalwork. The corresponding school for girls is in Stavanger, where sewing, weaving and domestic science are taught. For children who are academically gifted there is a one-year continuation course provided at a small state school at Aln.

Separate provision for the hard of hearing is a more recent development and is as yet fairly limited. There is only one small state school catering for these pupils which is situated at Vikhov, near Trondheim. Moderately hard of hearing pupils who live in Oslo may attend one of the three special classes attached to the ordinary public schools in that city.

Both in Oslo and in Bergen there are private kindergartens for deaf children up to the age of six years. These have been established mainly through the support of parents of deaf children. It is planned to establish a system of pre-school guidance through short courses for parents and advice from peripatetic teachers. At present, many parents of pre-school deaf children make use of the John Tracy correspondence course.

The provision of hearing aids is subsidised by the state, who pay a sum of 300 Kroner for the purchase of an aid for each child or adult requiring one. In the case of children, the balance of the cost is generally met by the local authority. Upkeep, such as the replacement of cords and batteries as well as the cost of repairs, is a charge that falls upon the parents. The aids supplied are those manufactured by a number of commercial firms.

Sweden has both a larger area and a greater population than either of the other two Scandinavian countries mentioned. The population is seven and a quarter millions, but as the area is almost double that of the United Kingdom, the density is only about one-fourteenth. Such a distribution is likely to make provision centralised and boarding accommodation essential in most cases.

Education for deaf children has been provided since 1809 and became compulsory in 1889. At present, deaf children are admitted to school at the age of seven years, but admissions are made only in alternate years, so that some children do not gain admission until they are eight years old. There is an eight-year compulsory period of schooling followed by a two-year course of vocational training. As in Norway, the education of the deaf and hard of hearing is under the Directorate of Special Education, a Department of the Ministry of Church and Education. Children with defective hearing are reported by the parish to the local school council which notifies the Directorate of Special Education. Arrangements are made by this office for hearing tests at the audiology centre at the Karolinska Hospital in Stockholm and for the appropriate placement thereafter of the children. There are four district schools for the deaf—in Stockholm, Lund, Vänersborg and Härnösand. Children who are categorised as hard of hearing are sent to the school at Örebro. Very backward deaf children, or those with multiple handicaps, may be sent to the institution at Mogard which also caters for adult deaf defectives. A two-year vocational course is provided for deaf boys at Vänersborg and a course for girls at Växjö. As an alternative to vocational training selected pupils who are academically gifted may be offered a place at the continuation school in Stockholm. This is a two-year course of study leading to the *Real Examen* (two years below university entrance standard). An interesting experiment in this school is that pupils normally attend only on alternate days, spending the intervening days in private study.

For moderately hard of hearing children a number of the larger towns and cities have established classes attached to ordinary elementary schools. Stockholm and another twenty-three towns have such classes with a total enrolment of about three hundred and fifty pupils.

Despite the late official age of entry to school (by British standards), many deaf children attend kindergarten from the age of five years. One of these kindergartens is in Boden, in the north of the country, and is state administered. The others (about thirteen in number) are administered by the municipalities.

Routine sweep-frequency testing is carried out by all counties at the seven-year-old age-level. Children who fail these tests are sent to an audiology clinic for diagnosis and, where appropriate, treatment. Pre-school children are also sent to these clinics for tests of hearing. This work was centred mainly on the audiology clinic at the Karolinska Hospital in Stockholm, but regional clinics set up in connection with the Universities of Gothenburg and Lund and at Örebro and Boden are gradually relieving the Karolinska clinic of much of the pressure. It is intended to open at least another four centres. A teacher of pre-school deaf children is attached to each clinic and she gives guidance to the parents of children who prove to be deaf. For those who live at a distance and for whom regular visits are not practicable, a course of one week's duration is provided at the clinic with hostel accommodation for the mothers. Recommendations for the provision of hearing aids for all deaf children who require them are made by these clinics and the aids are supplied free. There is a state inspector of hearing aids who is responsible for hearing aid equipment in all the state schools for the deaf and partially deaf.

GERMAN FEDERAL REPUBLIC

The Republic has a population a little greater than the United Kingdom but, as this is spread over a rather greater area, it has a lower density rate. None the less it is one of the European countries which may be described as densely populated as well as being highly industrialised. Before the unification of Germany in 1870 many of the German states had their own separate provision for the education of deaf children, the first being that in Saxony established in 1778. Germany was the traditional home of the 'pure oral' system of deaf education and many of the classic texts on the education of the deaf are by German writer such as Heinicke and Moritz Hill.

Since World War II the Republic has consisted of eleven states or *Länder*. Three of these, Bremen, Hamburg and West Berlin, are city-states. Each *Land* is responsible for its own educational arrangements under its own Ministry of Education. However, there is considerable co-ordination through a permanent conference of Ministers of Education of the different states. Amongst the committees of this conference is one dealing with special schools. In the three city-states and in Baden-Württemberg, schools for the deaf are under the authority of the Ministry of Education; in the other *Länder* they come under the Ministry of Social Welfare.

Compulsory education for deaf children begins at the age of seven and states provide either an eight- or a nine-year course. There are nineteen public and eight private residential schools for the deaf and fifteen public day schools. Most of the large towns have classes for the hard of hearing in their ordinary public day school system. However, these are under the authority of the Ministry of Education and therefore, except in the city-states, have no contact with the schools for the deaf which come under the Ministry of Social Affairs. This dichotomy of administration results in an impossibility of transfer from one type of school to another and to a lack of understanding between teachers in the two types of establishment.

To cater for deaf children under the age of seven years, rather less than half of the special schools provide *Kindergärten* where children may be accepted from the age of about three and a half years. Most of the supervision is undertaken by a *Kindergärtnerin* who is not specially qualified as a teacher of the deaf. The qualified teacher of the deaf may give only part-time instruction to the group each day.

More than half of the schools provide a compulsory four-year continuation course. Some of these courses are largely vocational and provide apprenticeship training. In North-Rhine-Westphalia, the school at Dortmund provides a more academic course with a *Mittelschule* curriculum (save that one foreign language, English, is studied instead of the usual two). Several schools also provide what might be described as 'further education' courses. These consist of four-week courses for young workers who attend two such courses each year. About fifteen to twenty workers attend at a time and as far as possible they are admitted in occupational groups. As well as providing practical work where possible, these classes give theoretical instruction in various trades and occupations as a preparation for examinations as journeymen and masters.

No free hearing aids are provided by the states either for children or adults. Payment for a hearing aid is the responsibility of the parents, though necessitous cases receive financial help. It would seem that only slowly is the gap between audiological advances and education being bridged. This gap was probably created by the conditions of war and indeed it seems that most German schools have had to begin life afresh since 1945.

HOLLAND

Holland is a small densely populated country with no real communication difficulties. There are thus no physical barriers to a flexibility of provision and, because of its wealth and stability, no economic barriers either. However, in an educational system which encourages free enterprise and religious freedom, schools for the deaf and hard of hearing are provided, at least in part, on a denominational basis. Thus, of the three residential institutions, one is undenominational, one is Protestant and one is Roman Catholic.

The earliest school for the deaf, that at Groningen, was established in 1790 and there has been a continuous tradition since then of steady growth and enlightened development based mainly on an oral method of education.

There is no compulsory system of notification of deafness in Holland, but despite this a large percentage of deaf children are identified quite early in life and may begin in a kindergarten class at as early as two and a half years of age. Education does not become compulsory until the age of seven years and a minimum course of eight years is obligatory. As well as the provision of kindergarten classes there is a growing extension of guidance to the parents of deaf children who are of pre-school age.

Of the residential institutions at Groningen, Voorburg and St Michielsgestel, the first named has gradually moved away in the last few years from a residential system to the establishment of foster homes for the children who are unable to travel daily. This principle applies to the day schools in Amsterdam and Rotterdam which have a considerable number of children on the rolls whose homes are outside the municipal boundaries and the possibilities of daily travel. There are more than twenty schools for the hard of hearing at Nijmegen, Eindhoven, Utrecht, Amsterdam and other cities. The minimum size of such schools is twenty-five pupils and many have considerably more than this number.

The Roman Catholic schools are organised into an association which is planned to cater for all ages and types of deaf and hard of hearing children of that faith. The residential school at St Michielsgestel takes all the deaf pupils whilst the hard of hearing pupils attend one of the eight area schools established in some of the larger towns such as Eindhoven and Nijmegen.

The Dutch schools follow a system whereby a more advanced secondary course for the abler pupils is established within each school. Instead of moving the pupils out to a special secondary school or continuation school, the selected pupils are formed into special classes following a normal middle school programme aimed at the examination for the U.L.O. certificate (*Uitgebreid Lager Onderwijs* or Higher Primary School). The syllabus for this examination involves the study of a second language which in most schools for the deaf appears to be English. Vocational training is given to all pupils in the three boarding schools up to the age of eighteen years. In the day schools it is generally organised outside the special school but in co-operation with it.

The provision of hearing aids is made on somewhat similar lines to that in Norway. The state provides a flat contribution of 250 fl. and the balance (somewhere in the region of 80 fl.) has to be met by the parents.

FRANCE

France, with an area three and a half times that of England and Wales, has a population of approximately the same size and therefore a density that is correspondingly lower. There is, too, a strong tradition of an educational system uniformly and centrally directed. It could therefore be expected that in France there is less likelihood of finding experiments in provision based on local ideas and enthusiasm, nor would one expect to find day schools except in the larger cities. In fact, these expectations are fulfilled and, it is not unfair to suggest, there is a well-organised uniform provision for children with impaired hearing which reflects a certain traditionalism and rigidity in its application.

It was in France, however, in 1760 that the first school for deaf children was established by the Abbé de l'Epée. The silent method of education which he introduced remained the official basis of education until 1880 and unofficially continued for some time thereafter. Such evidence as is at present available, however, suggests that schools for the deaf in France are now no less oral in their methods than those in most other Western countries. Education for the blind and deaf became compulsory in France in 1884. At present it is obligatory from six to fourteen years and thereafter pupils may follow a vocational training course for a further four years. Schools are of two types—public institutions and private institutions. The former consist of four national institutions (at Paris, Bordeaux, Chambéry and Metz) and three departmental institutions (at Asnières, Clermont-Ferrand and Ronchin). There are thirty-two private institutions which are mainly denominational in character. The national and private institutions are under the control of the Ministry of Health whilst the departmental institutions are under the Ministry of Education. Despite the fact that the statutory age of admission is six, many institutions admit children to kindergarten at the age of three and a half or four years.

Children whose partial deafness is quite considerable attend the schools for the deaf. In Paris, Lyons, Strasbourg and Toulouse there are schools for hard of hearing children and of course many such children are within the ordinary public school system. There are, however, no special classes for hard of hearing children attached to ordinary public schools as is the case in many other European countries. The institutions for the deaf are mainly residential; the position in Paris, for example, being one-third resident and two-thirds day pupils or *demi-pensionnaires,* whilst at Asnières the position is reversed. The parents of resident pupils are responsible for the payment of board.

Audiology clinics for the assessment of pre-school children are held regularly in the public institutions and parents of children who are shown to be deaf are given advice and help. This help often takes the form of courses arranged to take place in the summer vacation. Other diagnostic centres have been established in hospitals.

At the age of fifteen years vocational training is begun. A wide variety of trades are taught such as book-binding, printing, shoe-repairing, carpentry, plumbing, gardening, welding and house-painting for boys, and needlework, dressmaking, tailoring, machine knitting, toy-making, rug-making and household management for the girls. After a term of experience in various trades the pupil then specialises in a single trade for the remainder of the course. Mornings are spent in academic work and afternoons in vocational training. This work leads to a Certificate in Technical Proficiency (C.A.P.) equivalent to those issued by trade schools for children with normal hearing, but omitting reference to theoretical proficiency. At the time of this transition to vocational training the most academically gifted pupils are selected to take an advanced academic course. This is known under different names in different institutions but it is generally equivalent to the *cours complémentaire* provided as a supplementary course in the larger elementary schools leading to a *Certificat d'Etudes*.

THE UNITED STATES OF AMERICA

It is not easy to condense an account of the provision for hearing-impaired children in the United States of America without over-simplification and superficial generalisation. In a country which has a population of 180 millions in an area twice the size of Europe (excluding the USSR), a population density of only one-tenth that of Europe, and comprising fifty-one states, each of which is largely responsible for its own educational provision, a unitary approach can be misleading. Despite this warning, an attempt will be made to describe some of the salient features and to make generalisations which it is believed are reasonably accurate.

The first permanent school for the deaf in the USA was established in 1817 at Hartford, Connecticut. This was based on methods developed by de l'Epée and Siccard in Paris and made use of a silent system of communication. Although this institution was regarded as a national one, quite soon other states began to make their own provision. After the middle of the nineteenth century, as new states were created, and added to the Union, provision was made for the education of deaf children by the establishment of state institutions, often quite early in the history of the state. Although there is a Federal Office of Education (within the Department of Health, Education and Welfare), control of its own educational system is vested in each state and a great deal of responsibility given to the local school district. Despite this devolution of authority there is a good deal of uniformity as well as variety in the provision. In terms of variety there are some states which make provision for their deaf children entirely on an institutional basis whilst others have nothing but day schools. In terms of uniformity the general pattern of the education provided for deaf children in state institutions does not vary very greatly and the compulsory period of schooling is the same for each state. The greatest dichotomy lies between the institutions which, in general, follow an oral method of education up to the end of the elementary school stage and a combined or simultaneous method thereafter, and the day schools and private boarding schools which adhere to oral methods, introduced into the United States in 1865, throughout the whole school period. It is true, of course, that some state institutions continue with oral methods at the high school level for their hard of hearing and deaf children who are bright.

Education for deaf children, as for all children, is compulsory from the age of six years. Most states require attendance for a period of nine years but in a few cases compulsory education is for eight, ten or eleven years. Whatever the compulsory period may be, the tendency has grown, largely engendered by economic factors, for children to remain at school for longer periods, and now at least three-quarters of American children remain at school until they are seventeen or eighteen years of age. Some deaf pupils remain until they are even older than this.

There are three main types of educational provision for deaf children in the United States: state institutions, day schools or classes and denominational and private schools. Table 5 below sets out the numbers attending each at the end of 1963.

Table 5

Category	No. of establishments	No. of pupils in attendance
State institutions	70	16,938
Day classes	297	8,755
Day schools	15	2,302
Denominational and private schools	17	1,373
Denominational and private classes	53	1,209

In very general terms it may be stated that the aim of the state institutions is vocational in nature and accordingly, for the older pupils, vocational training in well-equipped workshops fills a considerable part of the time-table. Trades followed include printing, carpentry, baking, metalwork, art, beauty culture, hairdressing and needlework. In the other types of school the aim is to prepare the pupils for admission to ordinary high schools for non-deaf students—either vocational or academic. The successful attainment of this latter aim varies very considerably from school to school, but that it can be achieved is made abundantly clear by the report of one school on its graduates which showed that of 225 graduates who had replied to a questionnaire only thirty had had no further schooling after they left the school for the deaf. (1) Of the others, 126 had been to high school, fifty to vocational or trade schools, forty-two to business schools and seven to art schools. Children from the New York City school for the deaf (Junior High School 47) have been going to ordinary schools over the past thirty years and in the last few years this number has averaged over 80 per cent of those pupils completing the school programme.

Pupils from the state institutions (and other schools also) may gain admission by selective examination to Gallaudet College in Washington, D.C. This is federally sponsored and financed and was established as a College for the Higher Education of the Deaf in 1864. Through a scholarship system education and maintenance is provided free. The College is now an accredited university with a roll of about six hundred students. The method of instruction is known as the 'simultaneous' method and comprises the simultaneous use of speech, finger spelling and signs and the use of hearing aids. As well as the normal undergraduate courses leading to a degree, the College also provides a year of postgraduate teacher training for both deaf and hearing students. The deaf teachers return to the institutions in which combined methods are used and this is generally true of the hearing teachers also. The influence of Gallaudet College on methods and curricula in state institutions is therefore very great.

In general, hard of hearing pupils are educated in the same special schools as deaf pupils. No separate provision is made within the special school system for these two categories except in a few of the large cities. In the main, if a hard of hearing child cannot manage within the ordinary school system, he must be educated in a special school. Such schools admit all categories of hearing-handicapped pupils although in some cases the hard of hearing children are taught in separate classes or even departments. In the case of smaller schools this is not possible and pupils with a wide variety of hearing loss are found together in the same class.

Although education does not become compulsory until the age

of six years, many schools for the deaf have a kindergarten attached, to which children may be admitted from the age of five years. Not many schools provide nursery education although a notable exception is Junior High School 47 in New York City where children are admitted from the age of two and a half to three years. Nursery education is being increasingly provided by separate establishments. In some cases, such as the University of Kansas Medical Centre, the nursery classes are attached to an audiology unit; in others they are provided by local branches of the American Hearing Society. Guidance for parents is beginning to be given by some of these establishments, but in the main the pattern is one of pre-school education for the children. Parent guidance is, of course, notably provided at the John Tracy Clinic in Los Angeles where regular courses are held for parents. This centre, in addition, provides a correspondence course in twelve monthly instalments and a nursery school for demonstration and experimental purposes.

Ascertainment of deafness, in the case of children below the age of six years, is usually carried out at university and other audiology clinics to which children are brought by their parents or referred by their family doctor or local hospital when there is a suspicion that there might be a hearing loss. Most states, however, provide routine screening tests for children of school age using a sweep frequency technique or sometimes single or double frequency checks.*

SOME DEVELOPING ASIAN AND AFRICAN COUNTRIES

Whilst the provision for the education of children with impaired hearing is relatively meagre in such countries, it is not without interest to look briefly at ways in which the problems of making that provision are being tackled. In many of these countries education for unhandicapped pupils is neither universal nor compulsory and, indeed, the extension of education is seen by these countries as one of the primary needs in their economic and political development. With the immediate tasks of overcoming illiteracy and providing a modicum of education for all their unhandicapped children, it is evident that such countries, however interested they may be in the needs of the handicapped, are quite unable to supply the funds necessary for providing schools and

* See reference (8) to Chapter 3.

equipment and training teachers to meet these needs. W. D.Wall (2), in fact, suggests that these countries would need to devote about 50 per cent of their national income to the educational service for a period of many years to bring it to a level comparable to that of the developed countries of the Western world. This figure should be compared with the 5 per cent of a very much greater annual national income at present devoted to education in the United Kingdom.

In addition to this lack of finance there are in many of these countries a number of other factors which make this provision a far from straightforward task. In the first place, teaching as a career is not particularly attractive. Status and salary are not high in comparison with what is attainable in other professions, so that the better educated members of the community seek employment elsewhere. Educating handicapped children is apparently even less attractive than other teaching posts so that even those who enter the teaching profession with a good educational background prefer to teach unhandicapped pupils. Training facilities are not usually available locally and, when funds permit, most developing countries look to Great Britain, the United States or, to a lesser extent, Australia to train their teachers of the deaf. Commonwealth Bursaries and awards under the Colombo Plan have helped to facilitate this in some measure. Where funds do not permit, however, teachers serve a period of observation and apprenticeship locally which neither develops their own educational standards nor leads to any precise form of training. Malaya, for example, having sent teachers to England for a number of years has now at least fifteen teachers who have obtained the Certificate for Teachers of the Deaf from Manchester University. It is now proposed, and indeed the plan has already been put into operation, to develop a national training programme, making use of the services of a Malayan teacher qualified in the above way who has also obtained a Diploma in Audiology as a further qualification. Provided well-trained personnel can be obtained, this seems clearly to be the best way of meeting the needs of local teachers since the culture pattern to which the training is related in England, Australia and the United States of America is quite alien to the patterns in Africa and Asia.

Relevant also to the training of teachers as well as to methods of educating deaf children is the fact that in Chinese and some African languages some words are not distinguished phonetically but by differences in pitch or intonation. This means that several words may be written identically but the difference in meaning is given tonally or by the pitch in which the vowels are pronounced. The training, noted above, that is given to teachers coming from such areas for training in English-speaking countries does not, as yet, help them to deal with this very important problem and this further underlines the need for the establishment of national training as soon as suitably qualified teachers can be obtained to take charge.

A second factor which affects provision concerns the multi-lingual nature of many of the developing countries. In Kenya, for example, there may be as many as twenty-five dialects used within one tribal race. In Ghana, Nigeria and Malaya, as well as in other countries, there are problems of multi-lingualism. Malaya is trying to effect some standardisation with the introduction of Malay as official language as from 1967; Pakistan has two official languages—Bengali in East Pakistan and Urdu in West Pakistan. The problem of finding teachers to teach in such a variety of vernaculars is self-evident; equally apparent is the unsatisfactory solution of learning the official or standard language in school and then being unable to communicate in the vernacular at home. The extension of universal education and the gradual reduction in illiteracy which will result are likely to simplify the problem of communication amongst unhandicapped people in these countries so that its effect on educational provision for deaf children is likely to be a transitory one. On the other hand it is one that is unlikely to be solved for at least another two decades.

Other factors which affect the provision are of a social nature. In some countries the fact of having a handicapped child is regarded as being a stigma and a bad omen for the family. Consequently, deaf children tend to be hidden away and not brought forward when any survey is being made. Even within the village, their presence may be kept as secret as possible. In most developing countries agriculture based on the village is the main means of livelihood for a large proportion of the population. In such an economy child labour is important and deaf children, who can be trained by their parents to carry out simple operations in the fields, would be a distinct economic loss to the family should they be required to attend a residential school for deaf children some distance from home. The scattered nature of the population tends to make residential schooling the only possible way of providing for these children.

A further related factor is the lack of education of many of the parents, especially the mothers. This lack of education, which makes deviation from traditional methods and practices in bringing up children virtually impossible, also results in ignorance of the needs of deaf children and the importance of education to them. In Nigeria an English worker, provided by the Commonwealth Society for the Deaf, has not only taught a group of deaf children but has taken them about from place to place to demonstrate what can be done. This, of course, is merely scratching the surface of the problem in this vast country, but at any rate it has some local impact. Malaya has gone further in attempts to reach greater numbers of the public by use of radio, films and newspapers for making the needs and problems of the deaf more realistically known. Here again, of course, the effect is only upon these who at present listen to the radio, watch films and read newspapers.

A few brief notes concerning what has been and is being done in some of these countries may serve to illustrate methods by which some of these problems are being tackled.

In the developing countries in Africa, provision for deaf children has been of very recent origin, and in every case seems to have owed its beginnings to voluntary effort. Churches, through their missions, have been the prime movers although it has frequently happened that the government has come in at quite an early stage with some financial help. In Nigeria, the Methodist Missionary Society together with local social workers began a school near Lagos in 1957. A teacher, appointed to take charge of the school, was first sent to Manchester University for training and, after her return and the establishment of the school, other teachers were sent to England for training. By 1962 the school had grown to sixty-three pupils ranging in age from five to eighteen years, and there were over 100 children on the waiting list for admission. In that year the Commonwealth Society for the Deaf in England sponsored a worker, who had formerly been a lecturer at Manchester University. Initially, she started another school, surveyed the problems and tried to make known the needs and potentialities of deaf children. In 1963 she started to train a small number of local teachers to form a nucleus of staff for the expanding schools. These provisions, however, are in the western region of Nigeria only; so far no beginnings have been made in either the eastern or the northern regions. With a total population of 44½ millions it is likely that there are no fewer than 5,000 children with impaired hearing requiring special educational treatment, so that at present not many more than 2 per cent of the children who need it are receiving help.

In 1957 the Presbyterian Church in Ghana invited the Rev. Andrew Foster, a deaf American Negro, to start a school in Accra. Financial difficulties prevented a start being made until 1962, when the school was opened in Mampong. At present there are eighty pupils between the ages of six and twenty-five years on the roll. Since the population of Ghana is about six and a half million this means that about 13 per cent of the children requiring help are beginning to receive it. Last year the government voted the sum of £5,000 to help in the education of the deaf. This, of course, is a woefully inadequate amount, but on the other hand it must be recognised that with an illiteracy rate of 80 per cent the government has many more pressing claims on its resources. At any rate the money at least serves as a token in recognition of the need. A team, headed by a German E.N.T. consultant, is at present investigating the problems of deafness in the country.

In Kenya, a Society for Deaf and Dumb Children—a voluntary organisation—was established in 1958. It sponsors a diagnostic clinic for African and Asian children in Nairobi and is trying to promote schools in different areas where children will be taught in the vernacular. At present the only trained teacher of the deaf is a Franciscan nun who works with a small group in a rural area. Another teacher, trained in England, will also shortly be going out to teach in another district, whilst a beginning has been made, again under the auspices of the Commonwealth Society for the Deaf, to give some training to local teachers. The African District Councils are beginning to take an interest in the education of their deaf children, but efforts are hampered by the lack of trained teachers. Teachers are in short supply for ordinary schools: they are mostly Africans who have had a very restricted education themselves. At present only about 50 per cent of the unhandicapped children receive a period of primary education which is at most six years and often much less. In such a situation the development of education for deaf children will inevitably be slow.

In Southern Rhodesia, as in Kenya, there are problems of racial relationships which add another variable to the provision. There is only one school for mentally and physically handicapped white children and within this there is a class for deaf children. For African children the basis of provision is the mission schools. By mutual agreement, different missions cater for different handicaps and families move, when they can be persuaded of the importance of education, to the area in which the mission caters for the specific handicap of their children. The Swedish Mission, to which there is attached a qualified teacher of the deaf, is one of those which have made special provision for deaf children. These mission schools receive some subsidies from the government, generally in the form of the payment of teachers' salaries. Parents are expected to contribute what they can to assist in the upkeep of the school.

The developing countries in Asia have many of the same problems but, with a predominantly non-Christian population, have received much less help from Christian Churches than the African countries. In Ceylon, however, the first school for the deaf was established through missionary enterprise in 1912. The school, at Mount Lavinia, is now managed by a representative Board of Trustees with, since 1947, a Ceylonese Principal. There are 190 pupils, mostly resident, and the language used throughout the school is Sinhalese. The school is financed to a large extent by public subscriptions and donations, but the state pays salaries of teachers and gives a small grant towards the cost of apparatus. Parents pay what they can afford towards maintenance. Tamil-speaking children are catered for in a separate school in Jafua. In 1956 a National Council for the Deaf and Blind was established in Ceylon, and this body acts in an advisory capacity to the government. The Council also provides hearing aids for children as their funds permit. Since 1960 three more schools catering for both deaf and blind pupils have been opened in Ceylon under the auspices of the Buddhist Congress and in 1962 the National Council opened a kindergarten for children aged four to six years. There is no specific course for training teachers in Ceylon and the responsibility rests with the principal of each school to train teachers on an in-service basis.

Pakistan has five schools in the east and ten in the more popu-lous west. Although there are linguistic problems, the matter is somewhat eased by each part having its own official language These schools, which are relatively small, hardly begin to provide for the very large number of children with impaired hearing who need special help. There does not appear to be a great deal of awareness of the needs of deaf children for education, and both finance and teachers are difficult to obtain. The existing school were established and are maintained mainly from private sources, but a small amount of help is received from the Ministry of Social Welfare.

There was no provision for deaf children in Malaya until 1954 when their cause was sponsored by Lady Templer, wife of the then High Commissioner. This semi-official influence gave great impetus to the development right from the start and provision in Malaya has outstripped that in many other developing Asian countries. A boarding school was established at Penang and in each year since its opening two or three teachers have been sent to Manchester University for training. With this supply of trained teachers the school has been able to expand and educational provision has been extended to other parts of the Federation. At present, in addition to the boarding school, there are thirty-two classes of deaf children, each with a specially qualified teacher, attached to ordinary schools throughout the country. Although teachers are still being sent from Malaya to England for training, a local course of training has also been begun to meet the expanding needs of the work.

Malaya has four main languages—English, Malay, Tamil and Chinese—but as from 1967 Malay will become the official language. At first, because of the lack of Malayan teachers and books and the wide variety of dialects spoken, the deaf children at Penang were taught in English. Now a change is being made to Malay so that language teaching in the school is in a state of transition.

With the auspicious start to the school, and government recognition from the outset, it has been possible for developments to proceed more quickly in Malaya than in most other developing countries. Group hearing aids are now used in the school and a beginning has been made with the provision of guidance for the parents of pre-school deaf children. It will be interesting to see how the units for deaf children attached to ordinary schools work out in practice. If the experiment is successful it may prove to be one of the best ways of organising special education in developing countries, especially where there are not sufficient children in a region to warrant the establishment of a school. Not only will this kind of arrangement prevent children from having to go too far away from home but it will also enable the children to be educated in their own vernacular and have at the same time the essential services of a teacher of the deaf. Although units of this kind have many disadvantages, especially because of the wide range of ages, abilities, hearing losses and learning problems, it may be that in these particular circumstances the advantages outweigh those disadvantages. Their development should be followed with interest especially as it seems likely that other countries such as Kenya and Uganda are likely to adopt the same pattern.

REFERENCES

1   Numbers, M. E. (1960). 'Educational, Vocational and Social Experiences of the Graduates of the Clarke School for the Deaf'. *Modern Educational Treatment of Deafness* (ed. Ewing). Manchester Univ. Press
2   Wall, W. D. (1960). 'Some of the Problems of Compulsory Education and their bearing upon the Education of the Deaf'. *Modern Educational Treatment of Deafness*

3

Ascertainment, diagnosis and educational placement

We have been considering, so far, general arrangements for the provision of educational facilities for hearing-handicapped children; it will now be appropriate to discuss ways in which these children may be identified, their handicap accurately diagnosed and assessed and guidance given concerning suitable educational treatment.

SCREENING TESTS OF HEARING

Ascertainment, or case-finding, is most efficiently carried out when it is planned as a two-step process. The first stage is the provision of appropriate tests which will reliably differentiate between those who appear to respond normally to sound and those who do not. The second stage involves a detailed examination of those who have not responded normally with a view to obtaining an accurate measure of the extent of the impairment, if any. Testing at the first stage is usually referred to as 'screening' and tests and techniques have been evolved for use with children at different levels of maturation.

Criteria for satisfactory screening tests would seem to be as follows:

1 All children with normal hearing, and no other handicap, of the age for which the particular test was designed should be able to pass the test; that is, there should be no false negatives.
2 Children with impaired hearing should fail the test; that is, there should be no false positives.
3 Implicit in the above two criteria is that the sound stimuli should be presented at a level not greater than the upper limit of normal threshold of acuity or detectability.
4 The test material and techniques of presentation should be appropriate to the ages of the children with whom it is to be used. This is partly implied in 1 above.

5 The test should be solely a test of hearing and the type of response required should not include a skill which may not be fully possessed by all children undergoing a test.

6 For economy of the tester's time the test should be brief if administered individually. A longer test is admissible if it can be given simultaneously to members of a small group.

7 The test should be capable of being administered by an intelligent non-specialist without the necessity of a great deal of preliminary training.

8 The decision as to pass or fail should be capable of being reached simply and swiftly.

It has been shown by some workers (1) that it is possible to make tests of hearing within a few days of birth. The present evidence, however, suggests that it is most likely to be the grossest defects which are detected and that the absence of response at this stage does not conclusively prove deafness. It is probably hardly accurate to describe these tests as screening tests and it is not until development has gone considerably further that it is possible to provide a test which can differentiate, with reasonable ease, a normal response to sound from an abnormal one. Such tests are based upon the growth of the ability to locate the source of sound: an ability which is reasonably well-developed in most children by the age of seven months. Screening procedures, based on the early stages on localisation, have been developed by the Ewings and explained by them in detail (2, 3). At later developmental stages, ability to comprehend speech is included as part of the testing procedure. The essential principles of these tests are, first of all, that the sounds used as stimuli at different developmental stages are of interest to children at that particular stage and therefore likely to evoke a response; and, secondly, that the sounds are produced at minimal intensity levels.

Screening tests for babies and young children, based on the above procedures, have been used for some years by an increasing number of local health authorities in Britain. Courses for medical officers and health visitors have been provided in their own areas and at the University of Manchester under the direction of Professor Sir Alexander Ewing. The Ministry of Health, in a recent circular (4), stressed the importance of the use of such screening procedures with all infants and pointed out that "ideally, auditory screening tests should be applied to every infant between 9 and 12 months". Since it was believed that this was impracticable at the time, it was suggested that certain groups of children should be considered to be 'at risk' and followed up until there was clear evidence that hearing was normal and that speech was developing satisfactorily. These groups included "all infants with a family history of deafness, and those known to have been subjected to any adverse prenatal or perinatal influence; children with congenital abnormalities, multiple handicaps, cerebral palsy and speech defects; and all retarded children".

The screening tests already described are those appropriate for children up to approximately the age of five years. For children above this age it is now usual to give a test based on response to pure tones. This test is described as a 'sweep frequency' test and the procedure is to hold the intensity constant and sweep through the frequencies in octave steps from 500 to 4,000 cycles per second (5). The usual level at which the intensity is held is 20 decibels re British Standard audiometric zero (6). This level is selected as representing the upper limit of normality in the acoustic conditions found in most schools. Subjects who fail at one or more frequencies in either ear at this sound-pressure level are deemed to have failed the test. Before such children are referred for the second stage of ascertainment, it is usual and desirable to give a second screening test to confirm the reliability of the first result. Normally this second test is a repetition of the first but in a current investigation the writer is using a variant procedure for the second test. This technique involves the presentation of a sound, of the frequency previously missed, at about 50 db, and, when this is responded to, the reduction of the presentation level in 10 db steps until a response fails to be evoked. The lowest level reached in this way is recorded as the approximate threshold level and where this is 20 db or below the pupil is deemed to have passed the test. This technique has so far worked well with over 3,000 children at the ages of five and thirteen, and thresholds obtained in this way have borne a fairly close relationship to those later determined in diagnostic tests. This procedure was developed first by Watson, John and Owrid (7) in work with mentally retarded patients.

A screening test involving the use of only one frequency was developed by House and Glorig (8) in 1957. Evidence presented by them and by subsequent users of the method, as well as by supporters of a double-frequency technique, has been somewhat conflicting and doubts have been raised about the wisdom of relying on what is undoubtedly a quick and simple test. In view of the high incidence of otitis media in this country and its attendant depression of low-frequency thresholds, it would certainly seem unwise to rely on a screening procedure which omits these frequencies. This opinion receives support from a report of a committee of the American Speech and Hearing Association set up to investigate identification audiometry which stated that there was a lack of incontrovertible evidence that the use of one or two frequencies only would identify an acceptable percentage of hearing losses in a school-age population. Accordingly they rejected its use in favour of screening at 500, 1,000, 2,000, 4,000 and 6,000 c.p.s. (9).

In order that any defects of hearing may be diagnosed as early as possible it is desirable to arrange for screening tests to be administered to school children as early as possible in their school careers. This would justify a test during the first school year, that is, between the ages of five and six years. In view of the high incidence of infectious diseases in the early school years, a second screening test at about the age of nine years would be desirable, whilst a further test at thirteen years or later would help in the early detection of otosclerosis, the most common cause of deafness in adult life.

Staff used to conduct sweep surveys need neither be audiologists nor trained teachers of the deaf. Intelligence, interest and a capacity for dealing with children are the main qualities required. Training is, of course, necessary and it has been found that a course of two to three weeks' duration which explains basic principles and gives supervised practice is generally adequate for this purpose. It is important, however, that it should be recognised by all concerned that those persons so trained are only qualified to undertake sweep testing and are not to be permitted to venture into the field of diagnosis without a great deal of further training. Supervision of the testing programme by an experienced audiologist is essential.

DIAGNOSTIC TESTS OF HEARING

When children have failed a screening test or when other evidence points to the possibility of a hearing impairment, it is necessary to undertake more thorough testing to diagnose the extent and nature of the hearing loss. One of the main objectives in diagnostic testing is to determine, in the first place, a child's threshold of hearing. This may be defined as the minimum sound-pressure level required to cause a sensation of hearing. Further objectives are to investigate how hearing functions at supra-threshold levels and to determine, as far as possible, the type of deafness from which the patient suffers. Diagnostic tests, there-fore, involve pure-tone audiometry and speech audiometry.

Young Children

For very young children pure-tone audiometry, in the usually accepted sense of the term, is normally impracticable below the age of about three and a half years, and only rudimentary speech tests of hearing can be given. Some workers make use of pure tones reproduced from a loudspeaker source in a free field, but here the possible effects of standing waves must be taken into account. Despite all these difficulties it is perfectly practicable to administer tests at this stage which yield highly significant information. At the earliest stage the techniques adopted are often described as 'distracting'. The response is therefore of a reflex nature and may take the forms of turning to the source of sound, pausing in or inhibiting an action, or giving other overt evidence of awareness of a sound. Emphasis has recently been laid on the importance of the state of attention in relation to the reliability of the response or its absence. The sounds are preferably those which are meaningful to the stage of maturation of the child and, as far as possible, are of known ranges of frequency. The sound-pressure level at which a response is evoked can be mea-sured by means of a sound-level indicator held close to the ear of the subject. The sound sources are rattles, chime bars, and other percussion toys whose frequency range has been established, and voice, including both vowel and consonant sounds. As the child matures, training is given to develop the type of response from a reflex into a learned one. The child is taught, in a simple play situation, to respond to a sound accompanying a visual cue and then to a sound by itself. In this situation the child learns to respond by doing something specific, such as threading a bead, putting one block on top of another, or manipulating some other repetitive toy material, whenever he hears a sound. The sounds will include voice, pitchpipes of known fundamental frequencies, chime bars, rattles and so forth, and the level at which a response is obtained is measured as before on a sound-level indicator held close to the ear. This technique is sometimes referred to as 'play audiometry' and it paves the way for introducing a child to pure-tone audiometry. The transfer from responding reliably to a sound produced by the examiner behind the child's back to responding to a pure tone emitted in an earphone is not a very great one and children of normal ability usually learn to do this from the age of about three years. 'Play audiometry' is not, however, just a means of preparing a child for later pure-tone audiometry: it is a reliable and valid test in its own right and thresholds obtained in this way compare closely with those obtained by subsequent pure-tone testing.

Pure-tone Tests

Once pure-tone audiometry becomes a possibility, it is essential to follow a well-defined technique for obtaining a threshold. A test of hearing being a psycho-physical measurement requires not only that the physical nature of the stimulus is known but also that the subject is confident about what he has to listen for and how he has to respond when he perceives a sound. It is helpful in the case of a young child (that is, between the ages of four and seven) to begin by teaching the child to respond to a simultaneous visual and auditory stimulus and then progress to a response to an auditory stimulus only, preferably using as a stimulus a sound analogous to a pure tone. When the child can confidently and reliably respond in this way, telephones are placed over his ears and he continues to respond in the same manner to the pure tones. The type of response required should be of the same type as noted in the preceding section (putting a peg in a slot, etc). For children over the age of eight or thereabouts, tapping on the table with a stick, block of wood or rubber hammer is a useful way of indicating a reponse. It is necessary to ensure that the child is not in a position where he can observe movements made by the tester as such clues are quickly seized upon to indicate the onset of a signal. For cerebrally palsied, or other children with a physical handicap, the type of response may need to be modified to suit their capacities. Thus a child who has poor muscular control of his hands may find it easier to kick his foot against the leg of the table or chair; the quadriplegic to make a head movement; the athetoid, seated near a wall, to strike his hand against the wall.

It is recommended that the tones are presented to each ear in the following order: 500, 1,000, 2,000, 4,000, 6,000, 8,000 and

250 c.p.s. This order is selected because in the case of severely deaf children hearing is often better at 500 c.p.s. than at sounds of higher frequency. The presentation should be brief—one to three seconds—and the interval between signals should be constantly varied. Since a threshold obtained when descending from audible to inaudible sounds may be different from that obtained when ascending from inaudible to audible sounds, it is necessary to decide which of these thresholds is the more acceptable. It is generally agreed that the latter is the more constant and significant level and it is accordingly recommended that this should be the threshold to be ascertained. The procedure (10) for obtaining this threshold is to begin with a signal well above threshold so that the subject is aware of the tone he is listening for and then, when a reliable response has been obtained at this level, to attentuate the tone in 10-decibel steps until the subject ceases to respond. From this point the intensity is increased in 5-db steps until a response is obtained whereupon the tone is attenuated by 10 db and again brought up in 5-db steps until a response is given. The lowest level at which a response is obtained in at least two-thirds of the presentations is taken to be the threshold for that frequency. As a threshold is obtained at each frequency the information is recorded on an audiogram form and the levels at each frequency joined to form a graph for each ear (Figure 1).

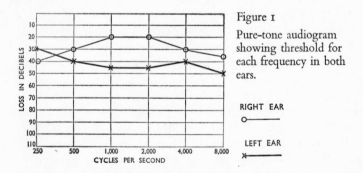

Figure 1

Pure-tone audiogram showing threshold for each frequency in both ears.

RIGHT EAR
o———

LEFT EAR
x———

When thresholds have been obtained for pure tones by air conduction it is necessary to find similar levels for bone-conducted sound. The procedure for bone conduction testing will be outlined next in this narrative, but it should be pointed out that in practice it is highly desirable to give most children a break between air and bone conduction testing to prevent incipient fatigue from affecting the results. A practice that has been found workable is to interpolate speech tests of hearing between air and bone conduction pure-tone testing. The change in stimulus and response usually serves the purpose of maintaining interest without the risk of fatigue.

It is not our purpose here to describe the process of hearing by bone conduction (11) and it will suffice to recall the fact that any stimulation of the bones of the skull will stimulate both cochleas. In the usual procedure in bone conduction testing the vibrator is placed on the mastoid process of the ear under test, but it is unwise to assume that it is only the cochlea on that side which will be stimulated by a signal from the vibrator since there is virtually no loss 'across the head'. The better ear should be tested first and a simple way of determining the better ear, when the evidence is not clear-cut from the air conduction thresholds, is to administer an audiometric Weber test. In this test the bone conduction vibrator is placed in the centre of the forehead and the subject is asked to state whether the sound is heard centrally or laterally and, if the latter, on which side. This test should be given at 500, 1,000, 2,000 and 4,000 c.p.s. If there is lateralisation, the ear to which the sound has lateralised should be tested first and it is not essential to mask the other ear at this point. When this has been completed the first ear is masked and threshold obtained in the other ear. If there is no clear-cut lateralisation it is necessary to mask each ear in turn whilst the contralateral ear is under test. Masking is often a source of confusion to testers especially with regard to the levels necessary. These are determined by the type of masking sound used (white noise or narrow band) and by the kind of receiver through which it is transmitted (external or insert). The main aim in masking is to adjust the amount so that a stable threshold is obtained in the ear under test, that is, one that does not increase or decrease with each change in the intensity level of the masking sound (12). Narrow band masking noises are more effective than wide band or white noise and used in conjunction with insert receivers make it possible to use lower levels of masking noise. An alternative method, using a narrow band noise and an insert receiver, is to place the vibrator on the centre of the forehead and the insert receiver in one ear. The response will then be an indication of hearing in the unmasked ear and when this has been determined the receiver is transferred to the opposite ear, the vibrator left in the same

position and the test repeated for the other ear. Since bone conduction readings on audiometers are standardised on the positioning of the vibrator on the mastoid process, this alternative
placement entails the establishment of a new zero for normal
threshold.

The bone conduction readings thus obtained are plotted on the
audiogram form relative to the air conduction threshold readings
(see Figure 2).

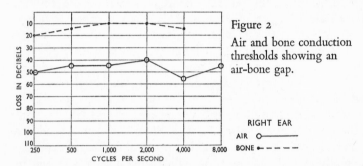

Figure 2

Air and bone conduction
thresholds showing an
air-bone gap.

RIGHT EAR

AIR   ○――――――

BONE ●― ― ― ―

A comparison of the two thresholds gives some indication of
the type of deafness. When bone conduction thresholds are
normal and air thresholds are depressed, there is likely to be a
conductive loss and the possibilities of medical or surgical treatment should be investigated. When air and bone conduction
thresholds are fairly close to each other, the loss is likely to be
sensory-neural in nature. In some cases there is a considerable
'air-bone' gap at the lower frequencies but the gap narrows as
the frequencies rise: these cases are often described as indicating
a mixed deafness. The audiogram, therefore, is valuable to the
otologist as an aid to diagnosis, although he naturally requires
much more information based on case history and clinical
examination to supplement it. When used in conjunction with
speech audiometry the results of a pure-tone test can serve as a
valuable guide to a decision about the provision of a hearing aid
and the benefits likely to be obtained from amplification. Since
the frequencies most important for the recognition of speech
sounds are 500, 1,000 and 2,000 c.p.s., hearing loss at these
frequencies should correlate fairly closely with scores obtained
in speech tests of hearing. Pure-tone tests of different kinds can
also be used for the investigation of other hearing problems such
as recruitment, acoustic trauma and functional deafness.

Speech Tests

Reference has already been made to the use of voice in diagnostic tests for pre-school children. Here, by means of a sound-level indicator, it is possible to assess quite accurately threshold of acuity for voice and also to what extent there is comprehension of speech and at what level. For children who have developed a moderate vocabulary the Kendall Toy Test (K. T. Test) was developed by Dr D. C. Kendall working in the Department of the Deaf, Manchester University. This test involves the ability to recognise some simple objects by name and to discriminate between these objects when, as in some cases, the names contain the same vowels but different initial or final consonants. Essentially, the test consists of three lists containing ten monosyllables each. Within each list there is a range of the most common vowels and diphthongs in conjunction with consonants which have a high degree of frequency of use. The child is required to point to the appropriate toy when he hears the stimulus phrase: "Show me the ...". To lessen the possibility of a chance response, especially towards the end of the list, an additional five toys are placed beside the ten test items, but either they are not asked for or are not scored. Such a test not only helps to establish the level at which a child can discriminate simple words but when, as is usual, the lists are presented at different sound-pressure levels, the effect of amplification upon discrimination is demonstrated. In order that the speaker may monitor his voice to a prescribed level within each list and to record reliably the levels at which different tests are presented, a sound-level indicator is used, held close to the child's ear.

Before discussing other tests to be used with older children, it seems appropriate to examine the criteria upon which speech tests of hearing are based, so that the tests may be considered in the light of these principles. In making speech tests of hearing we are normally concerned to establish at what level of sound pressure a child can hear the sound of voice and, thereafter, to discover his ability to discriminate speech at levels above this. It is often useful, in addition, to establish the level above which he is not prepared to tolerate amplified speech. Tests for the first and third items are relatively simple to administer: tests of discrimination present rather more difficulty.

When a child is sufficiently mature to co-operate in a pure-tone test it is a simple matter to follow this up with a test which involves a similar response to the sound of voice. One common method is to use the word 'go' as the stimulus word and to require the subject to respond (e.g. by putting a peg in a socket) whenever he hears it. When the child has shown that he clearly understands what to do, the sound-pressure level is attenuated in steps of 10 db from a level well above threshold, as in pure-tone testing, and, when it becomes inaudible, raised in 5-db steps until a response is again made. The criterion for the establishment of threshold is the same as for a pure-tone test. It is then possible to present the sound at increasing sound-pressure levels until the subject indicates that it is becoming too loud. The level above which he is not prepared to tolerate the sound of voice is termed the 'tolerance level'.

Tests of discrimination, or intelligibility, are best made using monosyllabic material. Because of the absence of contextual clues they represent more nearly a valid test of hearing for speech sounds than any other material save nonsense syllables. It is true that in English, or any other language, certain combinations of consonant-vowel or vowel-consonant do not occur so there is a small statistical probability of being able to assume the correct sequence by eliminating those which are non-existent in the language. This probability is not great, however, and is even less likely to operate with children than with linguistically more accomplished adults. Nonsense syllables make too difficult a test since the tendency is to try to perceive them as real monosyllables.

When using monosyllabic words with children it is important that the words are within the vocabulary of the age-range for which the test is designed, that is to say, that the children are able to recognise the words. If they are not, children tend to respond with the nearest known word in their vocabulary or, because they are uncertain of the word they hear, make no response at all. The tester is then uncertain whether the word has not been heard correctly or whether it has been identified as something else.

Monosyllabic word lists should be so constructed that the frequency with which vowels and consonants occur is as nearly as possible that found in current English usage. This is usually referred to as 'phonetic balance' and it is required in order that an assessment may be made of the subject's hearing for all the phonemes he is likely to encounter in listening to speech. Thus, if the short vowel 'i' (sit) occurs five times as frequently as the long vowel 'oo' (shoe) in current usage, it should occur five times as frequently in the list of monosyllables. It is this attribute of phonetic balance that enables us to apply the results obtained from such tests to the discrimination of speech in general. In order to achieve such a phonetic balance the minimum number of words required in a list seems to be fifty.

Since it is necessary to test subjects on several occasions or at a number of sound-pressure levels on the same occasion, it is essential to have a series of lists of phonetically balanced (or P.B.) monosyllables. These lists must be equal in difficulty so that we can assume that differences in scores represent differences in ability to discriminate in the varied conditions in which the tests were presented and not to inequalities in difficulty between lists.

Finally, the type of response that is required to these tests must be such as to ensure that it is hearing only that is being tested, and that the results are not vitiated by irrelevant factors brought into operation by the techniques of administration. For example, a test that involves writing the word that has been heard may, with some subjects, be a test of their ability to write words correctly as well as of their ability to perceive them accurately by hearing: or, for other subjects, a spoken response may affect the results because of the tester's inability to identify precisely sounds in the speech of the subjects.

The criteria for valid tests of speech discrimination may therefore be summarised as follows:

1 They should be constructed of monosyllables.

2 The words should be within the vocabulary range of the subjects being tested.

3 The lists should be phonetically balanced.

4 The lists should be equal in difficulty.

5 The responses required must not involve a skill which will cause the subject any difficulty or the tester any uncertainty.

With these criteria in mind we can now examine the various tests which have been developed to evaluate a hearing-impaired person's ability to discriminate speech.

The earliest monosyllabic word list tests were those developed at the psycho-acoustic laborities at Harvard and known generally as the Harvard P.B. Lists. These tests were used extensively in the United States but were seldom employed in Great Britain. Comparable tests were developed by the Medical Research

Council in England as part of a study which led to the development of the Medresco hearing aid. These, however, were in limited use. In 1952, Davis, Silverman, Hirsh and their associates at Central Institute for the Deaf, St Louis, devised a modification of the Harvard Lists known as the C.I.D. Test W 22. This test is probably the most extensively used in the United States but, because of the culture-tied nature of some of the vocabulary, is seldom used in Britain. Professor D. B. Fry of University College, London, has developed phonetically balanced lists of words for use in this country with adult patients (13). These have been used with considerable success to meet the requirements of a test of intelligibility of speech for deafened adults but their vocabulary is not sufficiently familiar to children to make them an effective test for use with hearing-impaired pupils under the age of about twelve years.

In order to satisy the criterion of familiarity of vocabulary a series of speech tests for use with children with impaired hearing has been developed by the writer at Manchester University (14). To provide a monosyllabic phonetically balanced word list within the vocabulary of children from about the age of six years and upwards, the Manchester Junior (M.J.) Lists were constructed. These are four lists with twenty-five words in each, with a scrambling of each list to give a total of eight tests in all. The vocabulary is simple enough, the lists show no significant differences in difficulty, but the phonetic balance is not complete since twenty-five words make too short a list for this to be possible. Within the limits of their length and the restrictions imposed by the level of vocabulary, the lists have as adequate a phonetic balance as could be arranged. The length of twenty-five words for each list was decided upon in order to avoid fatiguing children by having to listen to several lists each containing a large number of words. Having made this decision about optimum length, the phonetic balance had in some measure to be sacrificed. The pattern of response of normal hearing children to these lists is illustrated by the speech audiogram in Figure 3.

Whilst this test has been found very satisfactory in practice for children whose linguistic retardation is not very great, it proves to be of considerable difficulty for children with a more severe handicap. Since the test provides no guidance from context, the more severe the hearing loss the more likely is it that such an imperfect pattern is perceived that it becomes extremely difficult,

Figure 3

Speech audiogram
illustrating response curve
of children with normal
hearing to M.J. tests.

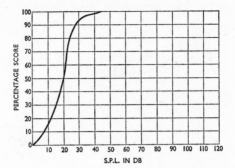

if not impossible, to recognise it. Moreover, many of these
children have accompanying defects of speech so that scoring
becomes extremely difficult and very chancy since the examiner
tends to be uncertain whether the imperfect spoken response is
due to faulty hearing or faulty speech, or both.

To meet the needs of children with whom these difficulties
arise, a test requiring a different type of response was devised by
the writer. This was the Manchester Picture Vocabulary Test
(M.P.). It consists of six lists of monosyllables containing twenty
words in each list. Each monosyllable is illustrated by a picture
on a card and each card contains six pictures so that the test
becomes one of the multiple choice type. One of the cards is
illustrated in Figure 4.

The lists of test words show no significant differences in
difficulty but, because of their length, are by no means completely
phonetically balanced. In construction, however, a careful
attempt was made to secure as good a balance as was possible
within the limits of the length. Contextual help is provided by
limiting the range of choice to one word out of six and the
chance element, which is never entirely absent from a multiple
choice test, is to some extent overcome by the inclusion of
pictures illustrating words with similar vowels but different
consonants and words with similar consonants and different
vowels. As far as can be achieved, therefore, within the scope
of six words and without making the test impossibly difficult for
very severely deaf children, the correct response can only be made
when enough of the phonemes are perceived to make the word distinguishable from the other words illustrated on the card. Chance
cannot be entirely ruled out and some guessing occasionally

Figure 4   Manchester Picture Vocabulary Test.

does take place, but it is generally clear to the tester when this is so and it has been suggested that when the highests core obtained by a subject at any level does not exceed 20 per cent, the result is ignored as there is a strong likelihood of the correct words having been obtained by chance. More complete directions about the administration of this test and the response of normally hearing children at different sound-pressure levels is given in Appendix A.

Since this test does not require a spoken response (the subject is asked to point to the picture) children with imperfect speech are not penalised nor is there any doubt in the examiner's mind about whether the response is correct or not. Thus, although it is a less searching test than the M.J. one, it nevertheless has proved to be extremely useful for pupils who are unable to discriminate words in that test.

Although it has been recognised that monosyllabic word lists are the most satisfactory test of discrimination, it is often useful to examine how children with impaired hearing manage with connected speech. It is true that this may be inferred from their scores on monosyllabic tests but a direct measurement can be helpful, at any rate with partially hearing children. For this purpose, the writer has developed a sentence test (Manchester Sentence Test) which consists of five lists of ten sentences each. The lists have been tested for equality of difficulty and standard-ised with pupils in the seven to nine age-range, having normal hearing. The sentences themselves (which are reproduced in Appendix B) consist of statements, commands and questions which are of the type normally used in primary schools, so that the material is suitable for children with impaired hearing at the primary or secondary age-levels. Scoring is simple and five marks are allotted to each sentence. The five key words in each sentence are underlined on the marking sheet and one mark is given for each key word repeated correctly.

Speech tests of hearing can be administered with a variety of instrumentation from the very simple to the extremely com-plicated. The more accurate the measure that is required the more refined must be the techniques and the more elaborate the equipment used. On the other hand, it is perfectly possible to obtain some valid information from simple techniques. The essential requirements are a means of monitoring the input, or a standardised level of presentation, and a means of measuring the output, or listening level. The best standardised method of presentation is by means of recorded speech since, with either disc or tape recordings, the material can always be presented at known levels and, of course, by the same speaker. If recordings are not available, or if their use is not practicable, live voice may be used provided it is monitored. A simple and accurate method of doing this is by means of a sound-level indicator held close to the ear of the subject or the microphone of the aid or amplifier which is being used for the test. By this means the speaker can deliver the words at the same level within each list and the lists at known levels for the purpose of making comparisons in ability to discriminate. If a sound-level indicator is not available, it is possible to use the meter on a speech training aid for monitoring purposes even when the aid itself does not supply the amplifier and output system being used for the particular test, so long as the microphone of the circuit being used is placed beside the microphone of the speech training aid. If a wearable aid is being used in a speech test it will not be possible to express the output in terms of db above a reference level but it is possible to record the score in terms of the different volume settings of the aid.

Although a rather more crude test than one using accurately calibrated equipment, a speech test with a wearable aid is none the less valuable in that it can be used to indicate the most appropriate volume setting in the conditions under which the test was made. Speech tests may also be given using a speech training aid or a group hearing aid. These, normally, have calibrated output controls so that the listening level can be accurately recorded. Their disadvantage is that they cannot be used for subjects whose threshold of detectability for voice is lower than conversational voice level unless they are used in conjunction with a tape recorder providing the test material. If the input is monitored live voice, subjects in this situation will hear the live voice under the receivers and thus render any measurement inaccurate. Moreover, most speech training aids do not allow of a measured output below 70-80 db. Group hearing aids are more satisfactory in such circumstances but only when recorded speech is used.

There are few commercial speech audiometers on the market and most clinics make use of their own calibrated system. One commercial firm, however, manufactures, for use with a tape recorder, a small attachment with a calibrated output into which the recorded speech is fed and into which the receivers are plugged. This has been successfully used for speech audiometry in schools as well as in clinics where more elaborate equipment is not available.

In making the recordings of material for speech audiometry it has been found that for normal clinical use the tests are best recorded and administered in good acoustic conditions. Later, it will be suggested that speech tests made or given in less good conditions yield valuable specific information, but in order to assess the functioning of a child's hearing in terms of speech, it seems essential that the factor of acoustic conditions is kept as constant as possible.

In work with hearing-handicapped children in this country it has been found that the two most useful pieces of information yielded by speech tests of hearing are the threshold of detectability for voice and the discrimination scores at different sound-pressure levels. This information can be recorded on a speech audiogram as shown in Figure 5.

Such an audiogram can be of help in deciding whether or not the use of a hearing aid will be helpful. For example, in a case where increase in amplification does not bring about greater

Figure 5

Curve A in this speech audiogram shows a typical response of a patient with a conductive deafness and curve B of a patient with a sensory-neural loss. The sound-pressure level at which the curve begins is the threshold of detectability.

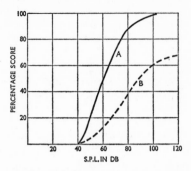

ability to discriminate words it might be taken to indicate, together with subjective evidence from the patient, that an aid was not advantageous. The speech audiogram is also valuable in showing the optimum level of amplification where an aid is found to be helpful. For example, in Case A above, the best listening level would be 90-100 db above normal threshold and in Case B it would be 118 db.

As well as their function in determining the state of the subject's hearing for speech and the advantage to be gained from using a hearing aid, speech tests of hearing can serve as valuable checks on pure-tone audiometry. In any comparison of thresholds it is, of course, necessary to make appropriate adjustments for differences in zero levels in the two types of test. Fletcher (15) has suggested that there is a close relationship between the pure-tone thresholds at the three frequencies 500, 1,000 and 2,000 c.p.s. and the threshold of hearing for speech. His single figure reference for purposes of comparison is derived by taking the average of the two lower thresholds at these three frequencies. It is expected that testers will be aware of the zero level of the equipment which they are using for speech tests and its relationship to audiometric zero.

The two cases illustrated in Figures 6 (a) and (b) are examples of an apparently perfectly reliable pure-tone threshold being shown to be quite misleading in terms of the children's ability to discriminate speech.

Child G. D. in Figure 6 (a) is a boy of ten years whose pure-tone audiogram illustrated below was very similar to those obtained on two previous occasions from another source. The speech audiogram, however, shows that his functional loss was much more likely to be in the region of 20 to 25 db. Child L. B.

E

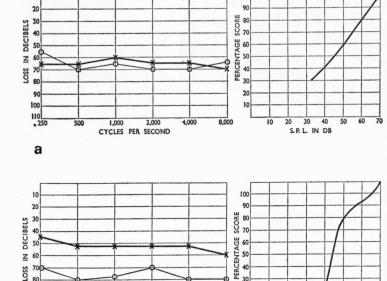

Figure 6 Comparison of pure-tone and speech audiograms to illustrate divergent information provided (a) and (b)

in Figure 6 (b) is a girl of thirteen years whose pure-tone audiogram indicates a severe sensory-neural loss. Speech tests make it very clear, however, that she is functioning as a child with a much less severe loss.

In some experimental work with patients in mental hospitals the writer has shown that speech tests can in some cases be more valid measures of hearing and hearing loss than pure-tone tests. In many cases where the subject was unable to co-operate in pure-tone tests it was possible to measure, within reasonable degrees of accuracy, the actual functioning of hearing in these patients and to obtain consistent and reliable results. In cases where the subject was apparently able to co-operate in a pure-tone test results were frequently considerably less reliable than those obtained from speech tests (7).

Other Diagnostic Tests

The above-mentioned pure-tone and speech tests of hearing depend on an overt response from the subject. In cases where the subject appears to be unable to co-operate in the tests or the results are inconclusive, as may be the case where there is gross developmental retardation and a diagnosis of impairment of hearing function as distinct from general backwardness is difficult to achieve, it is possible to resort to so-called 'objective' tests of hearing. These tests include psycho-galvanic skin response (P.G.S.R.) audiometry or, as it is sometimes called, electro-dermal (E.D.R.) audiometry and electro-encephalography (E.E.G.). The former test is based on a conditioned reflex response which, it is argued by some, is mediated at a lower neurological level (thalamus) than the cortical level which is involved in a voluntary response and therefore may not be a measure of the same function as the other test. Be that as it may, E.D.R. involves some subjective interpretation of the test results in view of changes in skin resistance that may take place during the test and are not due to the sound stimulus and consequently can only be satisfactorily undertaken by a skilled and experienced tester. For his reason, and because of the equipment required and the time involved, E.D.R. is not a normal clinical procedure and is generally only employed in cases where diagnosis by other means is not possible. E.E.G. is becoming an increasingly reliable procedure but its use involves elaborate and expensive equipment as well as interpretation of results by an experienced worker with neurological training. It, too, can scarcely be expected to become part of the normal clinical procedure, although Taylor (16) and others (17) have shown its value in differential diagnosis with difficult cases.

Attempts have been made with other procedures involving, for example, the relation of vascular changes to hearing, but even if these should be shown to be valid measures they are hardly likely to become part of the routine clinical testing of hearing. It is clearly valuable to have such techniques available for use in very difficult cases, but normal clinical practice is likely to continue to depend mainly upon conventional pure-tone and speech audiometry with the possible addition of new types of tests to gain additional diagnostic information and newer techniques for their administration.

EDUCATIONAL PLACEMENT OF CHILDREN WITH DEFECTIVE HEARING

In Chapter 1 the present provision for children with defective hearing was reviewed and it is into this existing provision that educational placement needs to be contrived. This provision, as has already been indicated, is a changing one and all the facilities are not necessarily provided within one area. Indeed it would be uneconomic and unnecessary for this to be done. Those who are responsible for making recommendations about placement, therefore, require to be cognisant of local provision, the alternatives available and the need to make the most appropriate placement within this provision. Where it becomes clear that this provision is inadequate to meet existing needs they also have a considerable responsibility in encouraging the local authority to extend their provision.

It is the view of the present writer that rather than attempt to classify children with impaired hearing, it is wiser to try to classify the educational provisions that need to be made. It is not always easy, as will be seen later, to make clear-cut distinctions between categories of children and there is always a risk in labelling a child and so directing him into a specific school or class because that is where children bearing this label are normally

Table 6

I.	Other services for deaf children with additional handicaps
H.	Other services for partially hearing children with additional handicaps
G.	Full-time special school for deaf pupils
F.	Full-time special school for partially hearing pupils
E.	Part-time special class
D.	Ordinary class+resource room
C.	Ordinary class+part-time help
B.	Ordinary class and consultation
A.	Ordinary class

educated. If we know the range of provision that needs to be made and, in many cases, is already made, then we can send a child to the place where his age, ability and aptitude can most adequately be catered for. A table giving a list of the recommended different types of provision is shown in Table 6.

The services provided by the different types listed above may be amplified briefly as follows:

A. *Ordinary Classes*

Children with impaired hearing who are sent to ordinary classes in this category will be those who require no special help of any kind. No special services are provided under this arrangement and the children who are appropriately placed therein will be those who are not handicapped in any way by the absence of special help. They may or may not need to wear hearing aids but it would be more likely that they would not need to wear them.

B. *Ordinary Classes and Consultation*

Provision of this kind generally involves special seating arrangements for the handicapped pupil and periodic consultation by a specialist with the pupils and their teachers. The specialist would be either an audiologist or a peripatetic teacher of the deaf. Consultation would cover maintenance and use of hearing aids, adequacy of communication, educational progress of the pupil and suitability of the existing arrangements to meet the pupil's needs. It is the kind of service at present rendered by some peripatetic teachers in the cases of pupils who are seen at approximately termly or half-yearly intervals.

C. *Ordinary Classes and Part-time Help*

This provision involves regular sessions of help either at the pupil's own school or in a centrally placed school or clinic. The number of sessions will vary according to need but are unlikely to be more frequent than twice weekly and if they are less frequent than once in two weeks they will tend to be little more than B above. The special sessions will relate to speech, lipreading, use of hearing aids and will probably be normally given by a peripatetic teacher of the deaf. They may also include sessions of remedial work in the basic skills given either by the peripatetic teacher for partially hearing pupils or a specialist in remedial work. It is likely that a peripatetic teacher of the deaf working for a local education authority will provide both services B and C. The category of the service will be related to the child's specific needs.

D. *Ordinary Classes and Resource Room (Specialist Teacher)*

This provision is possible where there are a number of partially hearing pupils in the same school. Each is attached to a normal class appropriate to his age and school progress and follows the ordinary class time-table for the greater part of the week. A number of periods, ranging from about three to ten per week, and allocated according to need, are taken with a specialist teacher in the resource room. These special periods include English, speech, auditory training and other subjects in which extra help is required and they are taken either individually or in small groups as other class arrangements permit. This arrangement enables children of different ages and abilities to receive help from one specialist teacher. The teacher can generally be responsible for up to fifteen children and as far as possible takes some lessons with ordinary classes. On page 24 examples of this arrangement already in operation were quoted although not necessarily under this title.

E. *Part-time Special Class*

Under this arrangement the pupils spend the greater part of the school day in the special class and take certain subjects, such as physical education, art and handwork and domestic science in classes with normally hearing pupils. This means that the pupils form a more homogeneous group than those in provision D. It is an arrangement that is similar to that already provided by many partially deaf units. In the case of older deaf pupils the provision may involve attendance at the special class for the greater part of the school day and for certain periods attendance at vocational or technical training schools for specific subjects alongside normally hearing pupils.

F. *Full-time Special School for Partially Hearing Pupils*

This arrangement is provided to meet the needs of pupils who require the whole of their education to take place in a class alongside other pupils with a similar handicap. It would include attendance at either boarding or day schools.

G. *Full-time Special School for Deaf Pupils*

In view of the clearly established principle that partially hearing and deaf pupils should not be educated together it is necessary to provide separate full-time education for these two groups. Once again, the provision may be day or boarding.

H. *Other Services for Partially Hearing Children with Additional Handicaps*

This will include separate schools or classes for partially hearing children who are mentally retarded, or maladjusted, or suffer from an additional physical defect such as blindness, cerebral palsy or motor disability. It may also take the form of additional special help by a teacher of the deaf in another type of special school, for example, a school for cerebrally palsied children.

I. *Other Services for Deaf Children with Additional Handicaps*

This provision corresponds to H above save that it is in respect of deaf children who may have additional handicaps.

In addition to this division of special provision into separate types it will be recognised that many of these types will need to be provided at each of the three main stages of school education: nursery, primary and secondary. Types A to C involve either no help at all or individual help so that no distinction needs to be made with regard to the ages of the children concerned; Types E to G may need to be provided for all three stages; Type D will be necessary at the primary and secondary stages and a form of this type of provision could be extremely useful at the nursery stage also. It would necessitate the services of a qualified teacher of the deaf, who was also a qualified nursery teacher, to be responsible for a normally hearing group for part of the time, giving special help to the deaf or partially hearing pupils as required. Types H and I will be needed at the primary and secondary stages and could be useful in some instances at the nursery stage also.

It will, of course, not be necessary for every authority to make provision for the complete range of facilities listed above. All should have B and C and possibly D also; E is likely only to be provided in the larger centres of population; F and G will be found only in large cities or serving a region; whilst H and I are likely to be required only on a regional or national basis. On the other hand, those facilities not provided by each local authority should be adequate in size to meet the needs of the authorities who will normally send the appropriate pupils there.

FACTORS AFFECTING PLACEMENT

Placement in the appropriate type of educational service will depend upon a number of factors, all of which are interrelated. First, however, the general principle needs to be stressed that this placement should not be a final decision affecting the whole school career of the child. It is to prevent the permanent fixing of labels on children that, as has already been explained, types of educational provision rather than types of children have been described. Initial placement should be in the type of milieu which best meets the child's present needs and there should be a regular annual review with a view to movement in one direction or another where the existing placement is not meeting the child's needs adequately. It should also be stressed that before considering the matter of placement an otological opinion should be sought as to whether or not the hearing disorder is amenable to medical or surgical treatment. If treatment is not indicated, or the early results of treatment do not restore normal function, the educational implications of the loss must be considered and the appropriate placement decided upon after consultation with a team of specialists which would include audiologist, otologist, educational psychologist and teacher of the deaf. They would investigate the following factors:

Hearing Loss

Information about this is obtained from the results of pure-tone audiometry. The techniques of making such tests with children have been discussed earlier in this chapter. Although it may reasonably be described as the most important single factor, hearing loss needs to be considered in the light of the other factors noted below which will modify the extent to which a child is handicapped by a given hearing loss. Some children, as the following examples show, with quite similar pure-tone audiograms have totally different needs as regards educational placement. The audiograms are shown below in Figure 7, but Case A is attending an ordinary school, Case B a partially hearing unit and Case C a school for the partially hearing. In each case these children are rightly placed but their placement has been decided by factors other than the degree of hearing loss.

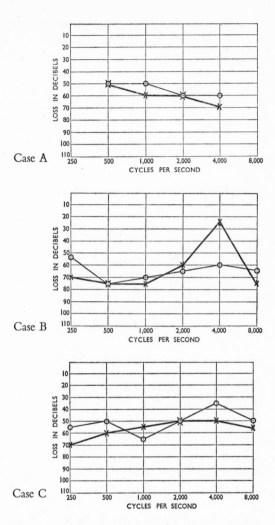

Figure 7

Audiograms of three pupils to illustrate placement

Case A

Case B

Case C

In general, of course, the children with the less severe losses will be found in the A, B, C and D types of provision, and those with the more severe losses in the D, E, F and G types.

Comprehension of Speech

Generally speaking, the extent of ability to comprehend speech is dependent upon the amount of hearing loss, but the relationship is by no means exact and may indeed show wide divergences. Different pathologies can create different patterns of hearing experience so that some children with moderate losses may find considerable difficulty in comprehension whilst others, with more severe losses for pure tones, may receive much more intelligible patterns with appropriate amplification. In Figure 8 below the pure-tone audiograms of three pupils are shown together with the scores obtained from speech tests of hearing. Although such wide variations in speech scores in children with similar patterns of hearing loss may not be typical, nevertheless they serve to show that the pure-tone audiogram is not a reliable guide to speech discrimination.

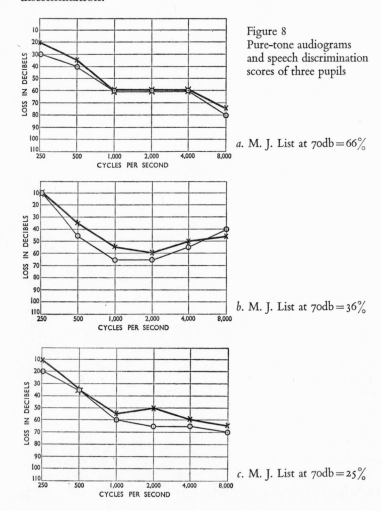

Figure 8
Pure-tone audiograms
and speech discrimination
scores of three pupils

a. M. J. List at 70db = 66%

b. M. J. List at 70db = 36%

c. M. J. List at 70db = 25%

In order to assess the ability to comprehend speech it is essential to make use of speech audiometry. The types of tests that can be administered to children of different age-levels and standards of linguistic achievement, and the information that may be obtained from these tests, have been described in an earlier section of this chapter. Speech audiometry, therefore, must be included in the battery of tests used to determine the most appropriate educational placement for a child.

These speech tests should be given under conditions of (a) unaided hearing, (b) unaided hearing and lipreading, (c) aided hearing and (d) aided hearing and lipreading. At the same time the tests need to be administered in acoustic conditions similar to those of an average classroom as well as in the good conditions of the clinic. This would include tests given at a distance of nine feet from the child since it is unlikely that a child using a wearable aid in an ordinary classroom will be closer to the teacher than nine feet. The extent to which a child can comprehend speech in a classroom under these four conditions will provide information on whether he will benefit from attendance in an ordinary classroom and the amount of help that may be expected from the use of a hearing aid there.

Linguistic Development

This is confined to an assessment of the spoken language of the child and his understanding of the spoken language of others. Use and understanding of language in terms of writing and reading should be considered under the heading of educational attainments. The assessment of spoken language should relate to vocabulary of usage (the words used by the child spontaneously), sentence structure, length of sentence and ability to express ideas with clarity. Understanding of the language of others can be assessed through testing ability to follow spoken directions or solve simple problems and the extent of the vocabulary of understanding (words understood by the child which he can define or explain). It does not seem that at present there is a complete battery of standardised tests gathered together as a single source which will give this required information. There are, however, a number of suitable tests and other information available which can give much help. Tests by A. F. Watts (18) and data from McCarthy (19) help in assessing spoken language, while the vocabulary tests from the Terman-Merrill revision of the Stanford-Binet Tests (20) and the Crichton (21) and Mill Hill Scales (22) are useful guides to the extent of vocabulary of understanding. Owrid (23) has developed a series of tests for use with younger children whose linguistic development is retarded.

These, and other similar tests, are a very necessary part of the assessment procedure in order that the stage in linguistic development reached by the child may be determined. The child who is considerably retarded in linguistic development will require a different type of educational placement from the child who shows little or no retardation, irrespective of the extent of their respective hearing losses.

Speech of the Child

This factor is related to the normality or deviation from normality of the phonetic patterns of the child's speech. The concern here is mainly with the extent to which speech is intelligible to others without taking into account the content of what is said. It is not, of course, easy to separate assessment under this head from that of spoken language since intelligibility is dependent upon content and structure as well as upon pronunciation. It is, however, necessary to assess pronunciation since the ease with which a child can be understood by others will have a bearing on the type of placement that is appropriate. Such an assessment will include voice quality, precision of articulation of consonants and vowels, intonation, rhythm, rate of utterance and the like. The different types of provision listed above will provide differing amounts and kinds of help in speech improvement.

Intelligence

An assessment of intelligence by means of standardised tests is necessary in order to decide whether or not the child is likely to make satisfactory progress in the type of milieu for which he otherwise seems suited. It may be, for example, that a dull child would be more appropriately placed in a grade lower than the type of provision which his other assets would seem to warrant. On the whole, the most satisfactory tests of intelligence for children who are likely to be linguistically retarded are performance or non-verbal tests. The best-known is probably the Wechsler Intelligence Scale for Children. Raven (Coloured) Matrices are quicker to administer but, though non-verbal, seem to give results biased in favour of children who are able to think in words. Other tests of the performance type which have been found to be useful with hearing-impaired children are the Snijders-Oomen Scale (24) and the Nebraska Test of Learning Aptitude (25). If it is part of an investigator's intention to obtain a prognosis of how well a hearing-impaired child will progress in an ordinary school there may, of course, be some considerable value in using a verbal scale or, better still, a complete verbal and performance scale so that the limitations imposed by any linguistic retardation may be apparent.

Educational Attainments

In school children beyond the infant stage it is necessary to find out how far they have acquired the skills of normally hearing children of the same age. The child who is backward in reading and/or arithmetic, for example, will need some additional help in these subjects. The extent to which this additional help is required is also a factor in determining placement. There are a number of attainment tests which are very appropriate for assessment.

Social and Emotional Development

Information in relation to this is important where there is evidence of maladjustment in a specific direction. It may be found, as a result of deviations in behaviour or in social or emotional development, that some children may need a carefully structured programme involving considerable dependence on the teacher, whilst others need a more challenging programme and greater independence. Some children may be persistent independent workers whilst others need encouragement and help at every stage. Information about this, obtainable through an educational psychologist, is relevant to the type of placement best suited to a child's individual needs.

It is helpful to summarise information obtained under the above headings on some form of record card. An example of such a record card which may prove helpful in indicating one way in which an attempt has been made to gather this material together is given by Ewing (26).

Summarising the contents of this section, it may be said that placement, to be appropriate, should be based on information derived from a number of sources. No one specialist is competent to obtain all this information, but each has a contribution to make to the overall picture of the child with defective hearing—his potentialities, weaknesses, needs and achievements. The final decision on placement will rest with the local authority who will require this complete picture in order to make the right decision.

Some examples of the information which was obtained in respect of a few cases is given below as illustrations of how placement was decided in these cases.

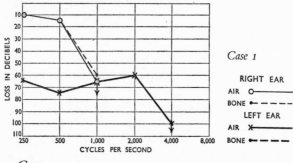

Case 1

Case 1

G.C. is a girl of 9 years. She could not discriminate speech when it was uttered in a loud voice but when tried with a hearing aid she scored 44 per cent. The cause of deafness seems to have been measles at 13 months and she did not begin to talk until she was between $3\frac{1}{2}$ and 4 years old. Her school report at the time she was referred was that she was slow in all subjects: that she lacked confidence and that if she could not do a thing at once she lost interest in it. She was approximately two years retarded in reading and her own speech was defective.

She was recommended for full-time special educational treatment in a school for partially hearing pupils.

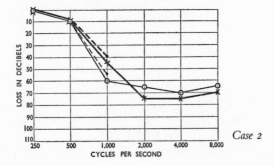

Case 2

Case 2

B.B. was referred at 9 years 7 months as a child for whom diagnosis was difficult. It was considered that he might be aphasic or possibly educationally subnormal. A hearing test gave the above audiogram and further E.N.T. and neurological examinations did not disclose the presence of any other handicap.

In speech tests of hearing he could discriminate with only 64 per cent accuracy at a level of 100 db. His own speech was very imperfect, his reading age was 5 years 5 months and his arithmetic age was 7 years 0 months. It seemed clear that the major handicap was high tone deafness and the resulting linguistic retardation. Accordingly he was recommended to have full-time special educational treatment in a school for partially hearing pupils.

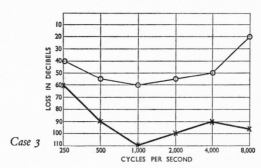

Case 3

Case 3

G.D. was referred for assessment at the age of 11 years 6 months. Her voice was monotonous but her speech was perfectly intelligible. There were no additional handicaps and she had been attending an ordinary school from the age of 5 years. She had been wearing a hearing aid for three years in the ordinary school but this did not appear to enable her to make satisfactory progress in school. When tested, her reading age was 6 years 8 months and her arithmetic age 8 years 4 months. On the Progressive Matrices Test she was classified as Grade III. In view of her low academic attainments it seemed wise to arrange for her to be transferred to a unit for partially hearing pupils.

Case 4

G.E. was first seen at the age of 8 years having had a history of impaired hearing from early infancy. Her speech was defective

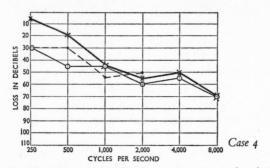

Case 4

but her linguistic development was only slightly retarded. The audiometric test showed her to have a severe loss for higher frequencies and very great difficulty in discrimination of speech. Her score in a monosyllabic word test was 44 per cent. On the first test she scored 60 per cent when using an aid in her right ear and 76 per cent when she could watch the speaker as well. After a year's experience in the use of the aid her discrimination score rose to 84 per cent without lipreading. She was recommended to remain in the ordinary school and have special help from a peripatetic teacher of the deaf. This provision seems to have been satisfactory and at the end of the first year of help her reading quotient rose from 89 to 94 although her arithmetic quotient has not made the same progress. Her headmaster reports that her written work in English is of good average standard for her class; that she takes full part in the school life, and is very happy.

Case 5

B.C. was referred for testing as a boy with retarded speech development and defective articulation. His general development had been retarded slightly but not very significantly. At the age of 5 years his adenoids were removed and speech therapy had been begun. He was first seen at the age of 6 years when audiogram (a) was made. E.N.T. examination at this time showed him to have enlarged tonsils and these were removed. A post-operative audiogram was made at the age of 7 years (b), but this indicated that there had been no significant improvement in hearing. Speech tests of hearing given in a free field at a level of 65 db resulted in a discrimination score of 88 per cent. At 7 years 8 months his reading age was 7 years 11 months and his linguistic development agreed with his chronological age. His mother thought that he was not doing as well as he might in school and

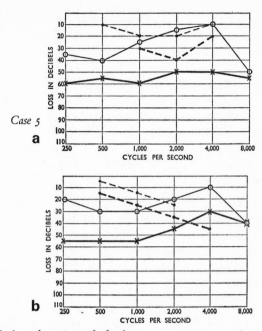

Case 5
a

b

he was recommended to be given help by a peripatetic teacher
of the deaf who would also give advice to the school staff about
the best ways of alleviating his disability.

Case 6

B.D. was referred at the age of 7 years 6 months because of
defective speech and behaviour problems. The paediatrician's
report contained such phrases as 'learning nothing at school' and
'seems to have little appreciation of spoken sound'. On simple
speech tests of hearing he scored 80 per cent at a level of 50 db
when tested in a free field and 60 per cent when tested at a

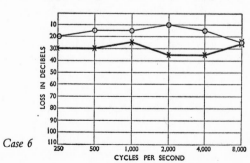

Case 6

F

whisper level. He co-operated well in pure-tone audiometry with the result as shown above. It seemed fairly evident that his scores on the speech tests were related to a very meagre vocabulary. On the Wechsler Scale for Children his Performance Quotient wa 58. It was concluded that although his hearing was probably slightly defective in the left ear this was not a major factor in his educational retardation. It was plain that a boy with such a low level of ability was not likely to make much progress in an ordinary school and it was recommended that he should be transferred to a school catering for pupils who were educationally subnormal.

These cases have been introduced to indicate the extent of the interplay of various factors in making recommendations about placement. They also serve to show in some measure the varieties of problems that are presented to the audiologist who in many cases has to act as collator of the information upon which the decision is based.

REFERENCES

1 Wedenberg, E. (1956). 'Auditory Tests on New-Born Infants'. *Acta Otolaryngologica*, 46, 446

2 Ewing, I. R. & A. W. G. (1944). 'Ascertainment of Deafness in Infancy and Early Childhood'. *J. of Laryn. & Otol.* LIX No.9

3 Ewing, I. R. (1957). 'Screening Tests and Guidance Clinic for Babies and Young Children'. Chap 2 *Educational Guidance and the Deaf Child* (ed. Ewing). Manchester Univ Press

4 Ministry of Health (1961). *Services for Young Children Handicapped by Impaired Hearing*. Circular 23/61. HMSO

5 Midgley, J. D. (1957). 'Screening Tests of Hearing in Primary Schools'. Chap. 5 *Educational Guidance and the Deaf Child*

6 British Standard B.S. 2980 *Pure Tone Audiometers*. Brit Standards Institute, London

7 Watson, T. J., John, J. E. J. & Owrid, H. L. (1964). *Measuring the Hearing of Patients in Mental Hospitals*. Unpublished report.

8 House, H. P. & Glorig, A. (1957). 'A New Concept of Auditory Screening'. *Laryngoscope*, 67, 661

9 *Identification Audiometry* (1961). A report prepared by the Committee on Identification Audiometry, American

Speech and Hearing Assoc. *J. of Sp. and Hearing Dis. Monograph*, Suppl. No. 9

10 Carhart, R. & Jerger, J. (1959). 'Preferred Method for Clinical Determination of Pure Tone Thresholds'. *J. of Sp. and Hearing Dis.* 24, 330

11 Naunton, R. F. (1963). 'The Measurement of Hearing by Bone Conduction'. Chap. 1 *Recent Developments in Audiology* (ed. Jerger). Academic Press, London

12 Hood, J. D. (1962). 'Narrow Band Masking in Bone Conduction Audiometry'. *International Audiology*, Vol. 1, No. 2

13 Fry, D. B. (1961). 'Word and Sentence Tests for Use in Speech Audiometry'. *Lancet*, 22.7.61, p. 197

14 Watson, T. J. (1957) 'Speech Audiometry for Children'. Chap. 12 *Educational Guidance and the Deaf Child*

15 Fletcher, H. (1953). *Speech and Hearing in Communication.* Van Nostrand Co., New York.

16 Taylor, I. G. (1964). *Neurological Mechanisms of Hearing and Speech.* Manchester Univ. Press

17 Goldstein, R. & Kendall, D. C. (1963). 'Electroencephalic Audiometry in Young Children'. *J. of Sp. and Hearing Dis.* 28, 331

18 Watts, A. F. (1944). *The Language and Mental Development of Children.* Harrap. London

19 McCarthy, D. (1954). 'Language Development in Children'. Chap. 9 *Manual of Child Psychology* (ed. Carmichael). Chapman & Hall, London

20 Terman, L. M. & M. A. (1961). *Stanford-Binet Intelligence Scale—Manual for 3rd Revision of Form L-M.* Harrap, London

21 Raven, J. C. (1961). *Guide to the Crichton Vocabulary Scale.* H. K. Lewis, London

22 Raven, J. C. (1958). *Guide to the Mill Hill Vocabulary Scale.* H. K. Lewis, London

23 Owrid, H. L. (1958). *Tests and Developmental Schedules for the Evaluation of Linguistic Development in Deaf Children.* Unpublished Ph.D. thesis Univ. of Manchester Library

24 Snijders, J. & Snijders-Oomen, N. (1959). *Non-Verbal Intelligence Tests.* J. B. Wolters, Groningen

25 Hiskey, M. (1955). *Nebraska Test of Learning Aptitude for Young Deaf Children.* Lincoln: Univ. of Nebraska

26 Ewing, A. W. & Ewing, E. C. (1964). *Teaching Deaf Children to Talk* (App. B). Manchester Univ. Press

SECTION TWO

EDUCATIONAL TREATMENT

4

The use of
hearing aids

The succeeding two chapters will deal with the education of
children with hearing handicaps and since the methods described
therein involve maximum use of the residual hearing of the
pupils concerned, it seems desirable, as a preliminary to this, to
describe in general terms hearing aids and their use.

GENERAL REQUIREMENTS FOR HEARING AIDS

It is not the purpose of this chapter to give technical information
on hearing aids which is available comprehensively elsewhere
(1, 2), but a few simple statements about general principles of
hearing aid design are essential to an understanding of the effective
use of aids and to the planning for the types to be used in different
conditions and for different purposes. All hearing aids consist
essentially of a microphone, an amplifier and a receiver. The
microphone changes the sound waves into patterns of electrical
current; the amplifier makes the weak current from the microphone stronger and delivers it to the receiver where the patterns
of current are converted back into sound waves. The amount of
amplification given by the aid is known as the 'gain' of the
instrument. There is, however, a wide variation in the gains of
different hearing aids, even of the same type. For example, Table
7 shows the range for a number of unselected aids of different
types.

Hearing aids, however, are not perfect reproducers of sound
and the range of frequencies amplified and the amplification of
frequency bands within this range are dependent upon the type
of components used. Small microphones are generally poor
reproducers of low frequencies and minature receivers are less
sensitive to high frequencies. It is therefore customary in wearable
aids, where small components are essential, to select microphones
and receivers which will supplement the weaknesses of each other
and give a reasonably smooth response. The overall gain of a

Table 7   Gains of hearing aids

Hearing aid	Number tested	Gain in db at 1 kc
Medresco (OL 575 receiver)	44	42—61 (mean=51)
Medresco (OL 675 receiver)	25	52—66 (mean=61)
Commercial A	48	37—78 (mean=62)
Commercial B	33	55—72 (mean=64)

(Reproduced from a report by J. E. John: by permission)

hearing aid at different frequencies is generally plotted as a curve which is known as the 'frequency response curve'. Very high quality reproduction would be indicated by a 'flat' curve within the range 200–8,000 c.p.s., since this range covers the most important frequency characteristics of the sounds of speech. The miniature receivers used in wearable aids have an upper limit of 3,000 to 3,500 c.p.s. so that there is an immediate limitation on the quality of reproduction as a result of this cut-off for the higher frequency components of speech. Examples of frequency response curves are given in Figure 9 below.

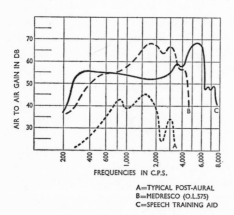

Figure 9

Frequency response curves of some hearing aids

A=TYPICAL POST-AURAL
B=MEDRESCO (O.L.575)
C=SPEECH TRAINING AID

Studies have been made of patterns of amplification which seem to be appropriate for a majority of hearing aid users. The findings of a study at the Psycho-Acoustic Laboratories at Harvard University, published in 1947, suggested that the ideal frequency range should be a uniform one from 300 to 4,000 c.p.s. As an alternative to this uniform response it was suggested that there might be a rise of 1 db per octave throughout the range with an alternative tone setting giving a slope of 6–7 db per octave. This committee also proposed that the maximum output should be 132 db with variant maximum settings at 114, 120 and 126 db. The gain of hearing aids should fall within the range of 40 db as minimal to 80 db as maximal (3). In the same year the Electro-Acoustic Committee of the Medical Research Council reported that the most useful response was one of a 12 db gain per octave from 250 to 750 c.p.s. with a uniform response thereafter or, as an alternative for patients with a severe loss for the higher frequencies, a rise of 6 db per octave from 750 to 4,000 c.p.s. (4). A later recommendation limited the response to an increase of about 8 db per octave from 300 to 3,000 c.p.s. and this is what is approximately aimed at in the present Medresco aids.

Commercial manufacturers of hearing aids have endeavoured to meet the needs of individual patients by providing aids with a wide variety of response curves and greater gain than the Medresco gives. These varying response characteristics are provided through different tone control settings or the use of alternative receivers. Many of these variants meet subjective judgments on the part of users as to how faithfully the aids reproduce speech 'naturally', but there is not a great deal of evidence that they enable the users to discriminate speech with greater accuracy. Indeed, a study by Hirsh and others (5) appeared to indicate that there were greater differences in discrimination scores between the same aids used on different days than between different aids on the same day. The authors of the study concluded that although there were considerable variations in the frequency response curves of the aids used in the experiment, these differences were not detectable by the usual measures of speech audiometry. These attempts to provide selective amplification are, in any case, generally based on patients' thresholds of hearing as measured by pure-tone audiometry, whilst the actual listening is carried out at levels a good deal above threshold. There is good evidence that in many cases of sensory-neural loss the pattern of a patient's loss at supra-threshold levels does not follow the same pattern that it had at threshold levels.

If, indeed, the 'best' hearing aid for a patient is generally a matter for subjective judgment on the user's part, and discrimination tests do not give a clear-cut evidence of suitability, it is difficult to see how an appropriate aid can be selected for a young severely deaf child who has no standards by which to make a judgment. Whilst it might seem that the reproduction of the higher frequencies, which are often deficient in severely deaf children, is unnecessary, a pilot study by Watson (6) indicated that some children whose hearing deteriorated very rapidly above 3,000 c.p.s. did better with an aid which reproduced frequencies up to 6,000 c.p.s. than with one whose response cut off at 3,000 c.p.s. It would therefore seem that to enable deaf children to acquire spoken language in part through hearing it is necessary to give them as good quality reproduction as possible. This may often be a matter of compromise, as will be discussed later, but the aim should certainly be to make this provision. With regard to the question of gain, it is possible to be a little more specific. An aid must be provided for deaf children which can give a sufficiently high level of output to enable the pupils to hear speech at adequate levels above their thresholds. Such levels are considered to be not less than 20 db and preferably 30 db or more. This requirement is, however, subject to the maximum level which an ear can tolerate without physiological damage, usually of the order of 130–135 db (sound-pressure level re ·0002 dynes/sq. cm). It should also be stressed that this requirement must be met when the input to the aid is not more than 65 db. In view of the importance attached to the necessity for deaf children to hear the sounds of their own voices, a matter which will be discussed later, and also in view of the fact that some deaf children's voices do not give an input at the microphone of more than 65 db, it is necessary for the aids to have a gain of not less than 65 db if very deaf children are to be able to hear their voices at the necessary levels.

A factor that tends to limit the maximum available output of an aid is the poor fitting of some ear moulds. When these are too loose they allow the escape of sound energy which 'feeds back' to the microphone and gives rise to an unpleasant howl known as acoustic feed-back. It is possible to provide moulds which do make an excellent seal and enable the aid to be used at a high level of gain without acoustic feed-back, but this requires very careful taking of impressions, the use of material for this purpose which does not shrink in drying and the careful manufacture of the mould from this impression. Boothroyd (7) has investigated this matter very fully and has given information on methods and materials.

Before discussing the types of hearing aids available and their uses, two other matters in connection with the use of aids require to be noted. The first of these relates to the acoustic conditions under which the aids are to be used. A hearing aid will amplify all sounds to which the microphone is exposed so it is important that, as far as possible, only the significant sounds which the wearer needs to hear should be allowed to enter the microphone. External noise should be reduced to a minimum through the appropriate siting and structure of the building. Internal noise can be diminished through the provision of noise-reducing floor coverings and materials fixed to the bases of movable furniture. Intelligibility of speech is reduced not only by the masking effect of these external and internal sounds but also by the effect of reverberation on the speech signals entering the microphone. Sound waves emanate from a speaker's mouth in all directions and the microphone receives not only those which come direct but also those which have been reflected from the surface of the room, ceiling, walls, floor, windows, furniture etc. If these surfaces are hard, a great deal of reflection from surface to surface takes place so that signals continue to be received by the microphone for a time after the direct signal has ceased. This continued reflection is known as reverberation and the length of time during which it continues is known as the reverberation time of the room. The provision of absorbent materials, skilfully placed on some of the surfaces and having varying properties of absorption for different sound frequencies, is the means whereby excessive reverberation time is reduced. In a speech test given to deafened adults John (8) found that when the reverberation time of a room was reduced from 0·7 seconds to 0·5 seconds their discrimination scores rose from 52 per cent to a mean of 70 per cent. This time of 0·5 second is considered to be a very satisfactory one for hearing aid users.

The second matter to which reference must be made is concerned with the distance of the speaker from the microphone. This affects the input level of the speech entering the microphone and, as distance increases, so that level drops. Experimental work done by Sivian, Dun and White (9) and summarised in Table 8 indicates the way in which this happens.

It should be particularly noticed how the higher frequencies are

Table 8 Effect of distance from the microphone on input level

Distance from speaker to microphone	6 in.	1 ft	2 ft	1 metre
Level (in db) directly in front of the head				
(i) Whole speech	80·9	75·1	69·7	65·4
(ii) Speech band 2,800–4,000 c.p.s.	86·2	75·1	64·4	55·8
Levels (in db) at 90° to the side of the head				
(i) Whole speech	80·1	74·7	68·0	64·6
(ii) Speech band 2,800–4,000 c.p.s.	82·1	72·2	56·1	48·1

enhanced when speech is close to the microphone and how rapidly their intensity diminishes with increased distance. The same frequencies are also very much affected by the angle between the source and the microphone. When an attempt is made to overcome the effects of distance by increasing the loudness of the speech, the effects of reverberation, especially in inadequately treated rooms, come into play and reduce intelligibility. Dale, in a simple experiment, has shown how intelligibility of speech dropped from 70·8 per cent to 64 per cent when moving from four feet to twenty-two feet in a well-treated room, whilst in poor acoustic conditions the scores dropped from 54·4 per cent to 39·2 per cent when the tests were given at these two distances (10).

Recognition of the significance of these matters is essential to the proper use of hearing aids. Their influence may be summarised by the statement that the most efficient use of aids is achieved when speech is close to the microphone (not more than six inches and preferably four inches) and the acoustic environment is a good one in terms of background and reverberation suppression.

TYPES OF HEARING AIDS AVAILABLE

Hearing aids that are in general use may be divided into three main types—wearable aids, portable aids and group aids. Into the first category fall aids which are worn on the body, behind the ear and in spectacle frames. In the second category are what are usually described as speech training aids. They may be mains or battery operated and are designed for one listener, or very occasionally two. They may have a single microphone or one each for the parent or teacher and the child. Group aids, as the name implies, are used by a group of pupils listening together and the mains are used as a source of power supply. These various types will be examined in a little more detail.

Wearable Aids

Most wearable aids used in the United Kingdom are still of the bodyworn type. Amplification is by means of transistors and with miniature batteries the aids are light and compact. The Medresco aid, supplied free under the National Health Service, is very commonly used. Its gain and frequency characteristics are noted in Figure 9 and Table 7. The gain is lower than that obtained from many commercial aids of the same type, but its frequency characteristics are good by the standards previously noted. The gain can be increased by the use of two batteries, thus giving a power supply of 3 volts. When the voltage of each battery drops to 1 volt it must be changed and at this point the gain is reduced by 6 db. There are many commercial aids of this type providing a wide range of amplification and frequency characteristics. The bodyworn aids are, relatively, the largest in size of the group of wearable aids and consequently are able to provide greater gain than the other types. For this reason they are the most useful type for severely deaf patients. They are generally worn under the outer clothes and so care must be taken to avoid the sound of 'clothes-rub' on the microphone. This can be minimised by covering the case with a material which produces little noise by friction, such as chamois leather, but generally metal cases are preferable to plastic ones for this reason.

Sometimes two receivers are worn with a single aid: the receivers being connected to the aid by a 'Y-cord'. This is not a binaural aid since there is only one microphone and a single amplifying channel. Used in this way there is a reduction in output of 6 db. Where there is symmetrical loss on each side the arrangement can be helpful, but where the loss is asymmetrical both ears cannot receive an optimum stimulus. Some audiologists consider that the dual stimulation provided in this way is of considerable significance whilst others have found no experimental differences in discrimination scores when a Y-cord is used.

Behind the ear, or post-aural, aids consist of a small case carrying the microphone, amplifier and battery which fits immediately behind the ear, connected to a small receiver fitting into the ear, or alternatively a receiver also in the case with a narrow tube leading the sound well into the external meatus. The gain of these instruments is generally of the order of 40 db and a typical frequency response curve is illustrated in Figure 10. An advantage of this type of aid is that since the microphone is at ear level it is particularly suitable for use in binaural hearing with one aid behind each ear. Worn monaurally it is less obvious than a body-worn aid and is therefore preferred by some on that account.

Spectacle aids contain the microphone, amplifier and battery in the frame with a tube leading into the ear. They may be used monaurally or an aid fitted to each side of the frame and used binaurally. The gain of such aids is generally about 30 db and a typical frequency response curve is given in Figure 10. Because they act as an effective disguise of the presence of an aid their sales tend to form an increasingly large part of the business of hearing aid dealers. At present, however, their output is insufficient to meet the needs of severely deaf patients.

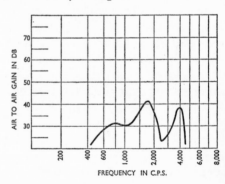

Figure 10

Typical response curve of a spectacle hearing aid

Speech Training Aids

These are portable aids designed to be used for individual work mainly. They may be mains or battery operated and the performance remains the same whichever source of power is used. Battery operated aids tend now to be more common because of their greater flexibility of use. The amplifiers are used with moving coil or dynamic receivers worn over the ears and good quality magnetic microphones. Such an arrangement gives a frequency response up to at least 6,000 c.p.s. with a curve similar to that illustrated in Figure 9. The gain is normally of the order of 60 db and the maximum output about 130 db. Incorporated in most British speech training aids are needles for monitoring input and separate output controls for each ear, calibrated in 5 db steps. The microphone can be held in the hand or supplied with a collar harness. Some aids may be provided with two microphones, one for the teacher and one for the child.

Group Hearing Aids

As their name implies, group hearing aids are used to enable a number of persons to listen to speech at the same time. They consist of an amplifier with multiple microphones and sets of receivers. The usual number of the latter is from six to ten pairs and they may be the dynamic type fitted externally or the insert type similar to those provided for wearable aids. Whilst the latter are light to wear they have the limited frequency characteristics associated with such receivers. Microphones are of the magnetic type: that used by the teacher is either on a collar harness or a desk stand; pupils preferably have individual microphones on flexible mounts attached to their desks. The maximum output of most group aids is of the order of 130 db and the frequency response is dependent upon the type of receivers used. Normally, a monitoring needle (or a 'stress lamp') is provided for the teacher and pupils to monitor the level of their voices. The amplifier has a gain control adjustable in steps of 5 db and there are separate output controls for each ear also calibrated in 5-db steps. Some amplifiers incorporate automatic volume control which limits the output when there is excessively high input. This may be done by means of peak clipping or compression amplification. Some group aids make use of miniature microphones, similar to minature receivers, which are mounted on a plastic boom carried from the headband of the receivers to a short distance in front of the child's mouth. This has obvious advantages in automatically resulting in speech close to the microphone but has the disadvantage of providing less good quality reproduction. Like so many other attributes of hearing aids it is difficult if not impossible to provide every requirement so that a compromise must be arrived at which seems best for the particular purpose in mind.

A further system of providing for group listening is by means of a loop inductance system. In this arrangement current from the amplifier is fed through a loop of wire creating in the area within the loop a magnetic field. Changes in this field can be picked up by a secondary coil fitted inside the case of a wearable aid and the current fed to the amplifier of the aid in the usual way and through this to the receiver in the ear. Input to the amplifier is supplied by a microphone worn by the teacher, usually in the form of a collar harness. Since a single loop of wire fixed round the perimeter of a room creates a magnetic field extending beyond the room, the wire is sometimes arranged as a figure of eight within the room which, properly placed, limits the field in a horizontal plane. It does not, however, prevent interference with listeners in rooms above or below the loop and to counteract this a commercial firm has produced what are described as 'slot inductors' which limit the spread of the field vertically as well as horizontally. Clearly, any size of loop may be used: either large enough to cover a hall or small enough to provide a field for a small group of pupils sitting round a table. Since inductance loops are used in conjunction with wearable aids the frequency characteristics and the gain of the system are those of the aids with which it is used. The microphone of the hearing aid can be used at the same time to enable the pupil to hear the sound of his own voice (he will hear the teacher's voice through the loop system) but under these circumstances the gain of the microphone circuit is reduced by amounts varying from 5 db in some commercial aids to 20 db in the case of the Medresco aid. To overcome the disadvantage of this some schools provide their pupils with a second aid to wear in the other ear so that they may hear their own voices more clearly.

An alternative arrangement to magnetic induction, involving the use of radio waves, is in use in Germany and Holland. The main advantage of this system over magnetic induction is that the teacher does not have to move about at the end of a long cable attached to the amplifier. The teacher's microphone is connected to a small transmitter which can be carried in the pocket. Signals from this are picked up by a receiver/transmitter which transmits them to a small aerial and thence to the pupils' wearable aids by means of an aerial suspended from the ceiling of the room. The amplitude and frequency characteristics of the speech signals received by the pupils are dependent upon the quality of their wearable aids and at present the position is no more satisfactory for the pupils to hear their own speech than it is with an inductance loop system. Despite this, however, one can look forward to developments in hearing aid equipment during the next decade which may confer great advantages on severely deaf pupils. Miniaturisation of electronic components, brought about by developments in the field of electronics, is likely to bring about new and exciting possibilities.

Binaural Hearing Aids

A true binaural or stereophonic system involves the use of two microphones, two amplifiers and two receivers. The microphones should be the same distance apart as human ears and the receivers placed in or over each ear. Binaural aids are commonly thought of in terms of wearable aids but they can be used in group systems also. Indeed a group hearing aid of this type was in use in a school for the deaf in England more than twenty-five years ago. In recent years much has been said and written about the advantages of a binaural over a monaural system, but whether the stimulus came from commercial companies wishing to double their sales of aids or from those who felt that a binaural system was in fact advantageous is difficult to determine. Although much of the support and some of the criticisms are the result of subjective opinions and badly designed experiments, there has nevertheless been a considerable amount of sound experimental work carried out in the last five or six years which throws some light on the benefits that can be expected from the use of binaural aids. Most of this experimental work has been based on comparing binaural and monaural aids in respect of discrimination scores using monosyllabic word list tests, in quiet and varying conditions of background noise, in speech reception thresholds and in ability to locate the source of sound. The evidence, on the whole, seems to be in favour of binaural aids for patients with losses of up to about 70 db, but this is by no means conclusive(11, 12). Jerger, Carhart and Dirks (13) suggest that there is a strong impression that advantages from binaural aids do exist but that the normal tools of measurement do not bring this out. They feel that the user is his own best judge of the advantages and in response to an enquiry found that users did in fact report some conditions in which binaural aids were particularly advantageous. Nevertheless, they felt that some users were committed to binaural aids from an "emotional conviction that two aids are better than one". Most of this work has been carried out with adult patients but

G

Groen (14) included a large number of children aged ten to fourteen years in his survey of patients with perceptive deafness and found that in many cases discrimination scores improved. Whetnall (15) working with pre-school children has described some cases where binaural aids were successfully used. She has suggested that the advantages of such aids with young children could only be assessed by observing changes in behaviour, particularly in the speed with which they learned to talk. Under the direction of the late Dr C. V. Hudgins, a longitudinal study of the response of pupils in the Clarke School for the Deaf, Massachusetts, to binaural aids was begun some years ago. Certain classes were supplied with binaural group aids for continuous use in the classroom and the progress of the pupils compared with that of other pupils using ordinary monaural group aids. Final assessment of the results of this study have not yet been published but it should provide valuable information about the use of binaural aids with severely and profoundly deaf children. It is in this particular direction that information is chiefly lacking and, as other investigators have pointed out, adequate means of assessment have yet to be developed.

THE USE OF HEARING AIDS

In order to be able to make the maximum effective use of the residual hearing of pupils it is necessary to know not only about the performance of different types of aids but also about the capacity of pupils to benefit from them. Information about this is essential for the class teacher and should be among the data with which she is very familiar. It can be obtained by making use of speech tests of hearing, such as those described in Chapter 3, in conjunction with the different types of aid available for the pupils in the conditions in which they are likely to be used. Thus, with speech training and group aids where speech is normally close to the microphone, tests should be made with and without lipreading to determine how much individual pupils can discriminate in these two conditions, and the optimum volume settings which will enable them to do so. With inductance loops the same tests need to be given but, since the volume controls of the aids used in this case are not calibrated, the optimum settings can only be given in relation to the numbered positions of the volume control of the aid. This also applies to wearable aids but these are used normally by the pupil when seated in his usual position in the room, say nine feet from the teacher, as well as when the teacher talks closely into the microphone, so that tests need to be given in these two conditions. When the settings for the different types of aid and the different conditions in which they are used have been determined, not only does the teacher require to keep a record but the pupils themselves should know them and be given increasing responsibility for ensuring that the correct setting is used. At first the teacher will need to verify that the settings are correct, but it is a valuable piece of training to place the onus on the pupil as soon as he is capable of accepting it.

Perhaps, at this point, it is necessary to discuss why it seems so important to lay so much stress on the use of residual hearing capacity even in profoundly deaf children where this capacity is minimal. One of the main reasons is that it can enable these children to hear the sound of their own voices. This 'auditory feed-back', or 'cybernetic principle' as it has been called by Huizing (16), is the main basis on which speech development rests in hearing babies and the evidence is (17) that it brings about a more rapid development of spoken language in hearing-handicapped children. Furthermore, hearing adds to the visual impression obtained through lipreading to facilitate comprehension of the speech of others. A number of writers, including Hudgins (18) and Clarke (19), have shown that even in profoundly deaf children there is a significant improvement in comprehension when hearing is added to lipreading. In addition to these reasons for utilising residual hearing, reasons which are indeed basic to linguistic development, there are other aims which it should be possible to fulfil. These include the use of hearing to bring about better speech in terms of voice quality, articulation, rhythm and rate of utterance; to reach higher levels of school attainment as the result of greater facility in comprehension; and to achieve better social and emotional adjustments through the provision of a direct link, albeit often a tenuous one, with other people and the world at large.

This conception of the use of residual hearing does not, therefore, envisage long periods of so-called auditory training, but rather implies the integration of aided hearing with the whole process of developing comprehension and expression and, through this, greater achievement and adjustment. This still leaves room for some periods for some pupils when hearing is utilised by itself as a means of improving discrimination, but such periods are of limited value, especially for profoundly deaf children. The value is probably in inverse proportion to the degree of hearing loss. The principle enunciated here, therefore, is one of looking and listening: the order of the verbs being reversible depending upon the extent of the child's hearing loss.*

For children who are partially hearing there is a much better case for pure listening practice. Here, systematic practice in learning to distinguish between first vowels and then consonants, so far as the children can be enabled to achieve the latter, needs to be given for brief regular periods. This practice would, of course, involve discrimination of words and not of isolated phonemes. There should also be lessons that help to improve intonation patterns and correct phrasing. As far as possible the groups for these lessons should consist of children whose needs and difficulties are fairly similar so that some pupils are not wasting time whilst others are trying to achieve what is as yet beyond their capabilities. Partially hearing pupils in special classes or schools will have to depend to some extent on lipreading to supplement their hearing, but efforts should be made to enable them to make the greatest possible use of their hearing. For older pupils it would also be helpful to give them specific practice in listening in poor acoustic conditions so that they will feel confident in knowing just what they can expect to get through their aids and what the limitations are before they leave school and have to adapt to life and work as adults in society.

The use of hearing aids by severely and profoundly deaf children is, as it has been described above, an extension of the child's resources as part of the overall learning process and it follows that the provision of types of aids should be as flexible as possible. Learning and teaching should not be forced into patterns dictated by specific types and arrangements of the equipment provided, but the provision and use of hearing aids should be considered imaginatively on the basis of the best educational procedures for members of a class at any given moment. Some compromises must inevitably be made, but these are acceptable provided that the teacher is aware that she is creating an appropriate learning situation and at the same time making the best possible use of residual hearing in that situation. Thus, whilst it is

* For further information about the development of the use of hearing and principles of 'auditory training', see Watson T.J. (1962), *The Use of Residual Hearing in the Education of Deaf Children*, Volta Bureau, Washington.

important to provide high quality amplification through aids which will reproduce speech over a broad frequency spectrum, it may be necessary to accept less than this by using aids which are more limited but enable the children to move about the room freely for the purpose of learning. The key word in this matter is the one which was used a few sentences earlier— 'imaginatively'. If a teacher has insight into what she is trying to achieve and imagination to devise flexible ways of using her equipment, then the advantages for the children will be immeasurable. Some suggestions of ways in which this might be done are given below in relation to the three main age-groups— infants, juniors and seniors. They do, of course, relate to deaf pupils who are receiving their education in special schools. More will be said about the use of hearing aids for partially hearing pupils in Chapter 6 in which educational methods for these children are discussed.

At the infant stage there will be a few periods during the day when the children are sitting down together as a class having a 'lesson' from the teacher. For the most part there will be activities in small groups either moving about the room, playing in a 'Wendy' house or standing or sitting round tables for various purposes. On this basis, therefore, a loop round the classroom will enable the teacher to communicate with the children wherever they are, but this by itself is not enough. Apart from the fact that they will not hear themselves or other children adequately unless they talk into the teacher's microphone, the teacher does not necessarily wish to communicate with all the groups in the same way or at the same time. This, accordingly, suggests that it might be desirable to have a few smaller loops in the classroom —one round the 'Wendy' house, one underneath each large table where a few children may be doing similar or parallel tasks, and one round each of a number of chairs in which a small group of children may be seated. Each loop would, of course, require its own amplifier and should have a microphone centrally placed for the children's voices to be picked up; for example, a microphone suspended over the centre of the 'Wendy' house a little above the level of the children's heads; a microphone screwed to the centre of the table with a 'swan-neck' fitting so that it can be pulled in any desired direction; and a microphone projecting from the wall above the level of children's heads beside the place where a group of chairs is placed or a rack of books kept. As the teacher joined a group she would plug her microphone into the amplifier of the particular loop. Such an arrangement gives the children maximum opportunities to hear their own voices. Whatever the position of the loop may be, it must be remembered that severely deaf children will be unable to hear the sound of their own voices well unless they are talking closely into the microphone. This being so, it is evident that from the earliest days the children need to be trained in this technique and the equipment arranged to give them the maximum opportunity of being able to do so.

At some period during the day, some at least of the class will be seated to 'listen' to a story told by the teacher or to follow a short directed activity. For this purpose a group hearing aid with four or five pairs of telephones would be the most appropriate equipment and could be set up in one corner of the room. This would be used when the activity was rather limited. More active group lessons would be better taken using the loop system. The advantage of using a group aid is that the pupils will hear the sound of their own voices and that of the other pupils better than they can through wearable aids and the loop system.

For individual speech work a speech training aid is also required because of its high gain, quality of reproduction and precise control of output levels. All this may seem to be a very considerable amount of equipment for one classroom, but unless there can be this degree of flexibility either the children will not receive an adequate auditory stimulus or the classroom methods will fall short of those appropriate for this stage.

In addition to those arrangements in the classrooms, a loop should be provided in the hall where such lessons as 'music and movement' take place. A tape recorder can be connected to the amplifier to provide the music and the situation can be controlled by the teacher talking into a microphone. Other rooms where group activities take place need to be similarly equipped.

The principles of curriculum building for junior classes will be summarised in the next chapter: they contain a proposal for smaller teaching and learning groups than the whole class and if this principle is accepted it will have a considerable bearing on the hearing aid equipment required. For the group lessons and activities in smaller groups that take place within the classroom, arrangements similar to those suggested for the infant stage would seem to be appropriate—a group aid in one corner, a loop to cover the whole room, and one or two smaller loops round tables and benches where small groups of children work. The group aid should have facilities for a pupil to plug his telephones into a socket at the teacher's desk, at the blackboard and at any other focal point in the room. This will enable him to hear the teacher and/or other pupils when he is away from his desk and also enable the other pupils to hear him in the same circumstances.

Individual speech lessons are important at every stage of schooling: at the junior stage they are critical and as much time as possible needs to be given to them, certainly not less than a short daily lesson. If group work is largely undertaken in preference to class work the possibilities for individual help with speech become greater. The speech training aid is the most satisfactory piece of apparatus for this work, although further developments of existing equipment are always possible. In Denmark, for example, use is made of a speech training aid which incorporates a pitch indicator where the display of the intonation pattern, although brief, is sufficiently long to allow the pupil to begin to try to match his pattern to the teacher's before the first display fades. A mirror is also included in the apparatus so that children can see as well as hear the patterns. When junior pupils become very familiar with the Hearing-Reading-Speaking Method (described in the next chapter) it would be possible to extend this to practice by the pupil himself. This would involve the use of a tape recorder connected to the speech training aid. The magnetic tape would contain sentences recorded by the teacher from the reading book used by the pupil. Each sentence should be recorded twice and the pupil, after listening to them carefully whilst following the printed pattern in the book, would stop the recorder and practise the sentence until he believed it to be close to the teacher's pattern. Repeated reference could be made to the latter and when the pupil was satisfied he could move on to the next sentence. Four or five sentences would be adequate for a single period of practice at the end of which the teacher would check on the progress made. One advantage of a method such as this is that it gives the pupil some responsibility for his own progress and reduces somewhat his dependence on the teacher.

At the secondary stage it is expected that a variety of courses will be followed. For many of these, such as science, technical drawing, art, crafts, domestic science and environmental studies, where the restrictions imposed by the use of a group hearing aid would be too great for the type of work to be done, the provision of an inductance loop in the classroom, workshop or laboratory is the best arrangement of hearing aid equipment that can be made. Freedom of movement is essential and the speech of the teacher, at least, can be heard adequately. For the more formal English and mathematics lessons, especially the former, a group aid is to be preferred. The pupils are likely to be sitting at their desks so that no external restriction is imposed by the aid and the advantages of this equipment over the others has already been explained.

The provision proposed at this stage would therefore be group aids for English and mathematics rooms (with loops as alternatives for certain types of lessons) and inductance loops in all other rooms. At the same time, provision needs to be made for a continuation of individual tuition in speech. Suggested methods to be followed are given in a later chapter, but as far as equipment is concerned the speech training unit is still the most valuable aid for this purpose. At this stage it is important that pupils should be given information about the working of hearing aids and their care and maintenance. They should also be aware of their limitations so that when the pupils leave school they are conscious of situations in which they are most and least helpful and can manage to look after their aids properly.

For severely deaf children at all stages, the use of wearable aids by themselves should be confined to work outside the classroom. Unless speech is quite close to the microphone most of these children are unable to hear enough of the sound of voice, if indeed they can hear it at all, to make the use of an aid worth while. Whenever it is possible to provide severely deaf children with an alternative arrangement which involves speech close to the microphone it should be preferred to a wearable aid, except in cases where teacher and pupil are able to talk closely into the microphone. For partially hearing pupils the position with regard to the use of wearable aids is not quite so critical, although even here it is necessary to be realistic about what is really heard by these pupils.

Techniques in the use of aids are, therefore, at all stages, use of the microphone close to the speaker's mouth, whether teacher or pupil, and careful monitoring of voice levels. With group aids and speech training aids devices are usually incorporated for the

atter purpose. With wearable aids and loops such arrangements
are not possible and the practice obtained by the pupils in moni-
oring their voices with group or individual speech training aids
needs to be carried over to their use of wearable aids, with and
without loops. As a visual guide for this purpose, one commercial company markets an independent battery-operated
monitoring device which is particularly useful for younger pupils.

REFERENCES

1 Davis, H. & Silverman, S. R. (1960). *Hearing and Deafness*,
    Chaps. 10 and 11. Holt, Rinehart & Winston, New York

2 John, J. E. J. (1964). *Hearing Aids*. Chap. 4. *Teaching Deaf
    Children to Talk* (ed. Ewing). Manchester Univ. Press.

3 Davis, H. *et al.* (1947). *Hearing Aids, An Experimental Study
    in Design Objectives*. Cambridge, Mass.

4 Medical Research Council Special Reports, Series No. 261
    (1947). *Hearing Aids and Audiometers*. HMSO

5 Shore, I., Bilger, R. C. & Hirsh, I. J. (1960). 'Hearing Aid
    Evaluation: Reliability of Repeated Measurements'. *J. of
    Sp. and Hearing Dis*. 25, 152

6 Watson, T. J. (1960). 'Some Factors Affecting the Successful
    Use of Hearing Aids by Deaf Children'. *The Modern
    Educational Treatment of Deafness* (ed. Ewing). Manchester
    Univ. Press

7 Boothroyd, A. (1965). 'The Provision of Better Ear Moulds
    for Deaf Children. *J. of Laryn. and Otol*. LXXIX No. 4.

8 John, J. E. J. (1960). 'The Efficiency of Hearing Aids as a
    Function of Architectural Acoustics'. *The Modern Educa-
    tional Treatment of Deafness*

9 Quoted in Fletcher, H. (1953). *Speech and Hearing in Com-
    munication*. Van Nostrand, New York.

10 Dale, D. M. C. (1962) *Applied Audiology for Children*. Thomas,
    Springfield, Illinois

11 Haskins, H. & Hardy, W. G. (1960). 'Clinical Studies in
    Stereophonic Hearing'. *Laryngoscope*, LXX, 1427

12 Wright, H. & Carhart, R. (1960). 'The Efficiency of Binaural
    Listening in the Hearing Impaired'. *Arch. Otolaryn*. 72, 289

13 Jerger, J., Carhart, R. & Dirks, D. (1961). 'Binaural Hearing
    Aids and Speech Intelligibility'. *J. of Sp. and Hearing Res*.
    4, 137

14 Groen, J. J. (1961). *Theory and Practice of Binaural Hearing*.

Proc. of 2nd International Congress in Paedo-Audiology, Groningen, Holland

15 Whetnall, E. (1963). *Binaural Hearing.* Report of Proc. of 1st British Academic Conference in Otolaryngology, London

16 Huizing, H. C. (1964). 'The Significance of Cybernetic Phenomena in Audiology'. *Progress on Biocybernetics* Vol. 1 (ed. Wiener & Schadé). Elsevier Publ. Co., Amsterdam

17 Pickles, A. M. (1957). 'Home Training with Hearing Aids' Chap. 4 (ii). *Educational Guidance and the Deaf Child.* Manchester Univ. Press

18 Hudgins, C. V. (1960). 'The Development of Communication Skills among Profoundly Deaf Children in an Auditory Training Programme'. *The Modern Educational Treatment of Deafness* (ed. Ewing). Manchester Univ. Press

19 Clarke, B. R. (1957). 'Use of a Group Hearing Aid by Profoundly Deaf Children'. *Educational Guidance and the Deaf Child*

5

The education of
deaf children

This chapter will be mainly concerned with principles, and methods will be discussed largely as illustrations of these principles. The education of deaf children is such a vast subject, involving an increasingly wide range of fields of related knowledge, that more than this would require a separate volume at the least. The titles of some post-war books relating to the education of deaf children give some indication of the scope and serve to highlight some of the most significant aspects of this problem—*Language for the Pre-School Deaf Child; New Opportunities for Deaf Children; Speech and the Deaf Child; The Teaching of Language to Deaf Children; Natural Language for Deaf Children;* etc. Language, therefore, and speech would seem to be the main topics that have been dealt with and they reflect the concern of teachers with those fundamental problems in the education of deaf children.

Before considering this matter further, however, some explanation of the term 'deaf', as used here, is necessary. No qualifying adverbs, such as 'severely', or 'profoundly', or 'sub-totally', are included in any official definition of deafness. As was noted in Chapter 1, the main criterion for describing a child as deaf is the absence of naturally acquired speech and language. An 'educationally deaf' child is, therefore, one who has had insufficient hearing from birth or very early in life to enable him to acquire language naturally. On the other hand, the term 'deaf' can be used in a physiological sense to mean having a reduced sensitivity to sound. A child who is described as deaf for educational purposes has, however, generally less residual hearing than an adult who is termed 'deaf'. The term deaf in this chapter will therefore be used to describe children who have not had sufficient hearing to enable them to acquire speech and language naturally and, in contrast to those who are described in the next chapter as partially hearing, have a very severe or profound loss of hearing. If an audiometric definition is required they might be said to be children who, from the age of two years or earlier, have had a threshold for pure tones (average 500 to 2,000 c.p.s.) in excess of 70 db. Such children form the major part of the population of special schools for the deaf, most surveys putting them between 60 and 70 per cent.* They are, however, by no means a homogeneous group and in any discussion of educational principles and methods this must be taken into account. The variations, in fact, are so great that a description of methods appropriate for deaf children in general is not much more meaningful than information about the 'average citizen' or the 'man in the street'. In a class of ten pupils in a school for the deaf the following variations have been found: age range, 8 years 9 months to 11 years 3 months; I.Q. range 88–123; one child with spasticity (not too severe), one child with a considerable visual defect and a cardiac weakness resulting from rubella and one child with severe emotional problems stemming from a broken home. This is by no means an extreme example and, lest hands be thrown up in horror at the folly of trying to cope with such variables in a single group, it should be pointed out that very many teachers are having to do just this. Methods, therefore, must be adapted to individual needs, and the successful teacher of the deaf is one who has a firm grasp of principles and has learned to make this adaptation instead of attempting to adhere slavishly to a rigid technique and follow an over-detailed course of lessons. These wide variations in pupils' abilities, difficulties and needs at least in part provide an explanation of the frequently observed wide variations in ultimate standards of achievement. The latter may also in part be the result of attempting to use identical methods with such heterogeneous groups as are formed into classes within schools.

The main problem in the education of deaf children is the development of language. Language learning takes place in infancy as the result of hearing, imitation and a 'feed-back' process. The absence of hearing or the existence of only small hearing remnants interrupts this cyclical process of learning and prevents linguistic development taking place unless special steps are taken to make provision for it in other ways. The education of deaf children is therefore a more fundamental process than the

---

* Murphy's sample (1) 60·7 per cent; Dale's sample (2) 71·4 per cent; Goodman's sample (3) 64·1 per cent (converting his use of Sabine-Fowler formula back to threshold readings).

education of normally hearing children or even of partially hearing children for it involves the development of the conventional symbols through which thinking takes place and their use as means of communication. These latter two groups of children come to school with a basis of language on which the learning processes that are part of the normal school curriculum are based. In the case of partially hearing children this basis may be, and usually is, an imperfect one, but it is already there and has facilitated mental growth in the pre-school period. Profoundly deaf children will not begin to acquire these conventional symbols which we call language unless and until they are given special help to do so.

Nowadays, fortunately, it is usually no longer necessary to wait until a deaf child comes to school before giving him appropriate help. As the result of the ascertainment of deafness in infancy and early childhood it is now possible to give guidance to the parents of those children who are found to be deaf. The main aim of this guidance is to enable the parents to help their children to develop an understanding of language and so begin to express themselves in speech. The principles on which it is based are the utilisation of natural routine situations in the home through which the child becomes aware of the meaning of simple language in clear-cut and frequently recurring contexts, and the encouragement of vocalisation as a means of expression and communication. The use of whatever residual hearing a child may possess is an integral part of this training and E. C. Ewing (4) has reported the very considerable progress that can be made through this. Stages in the development both of comprehension and expression have been suggested as successive goals to be aimed at and methods of achieving aims have been fully described (5). There is little doubt that developments in the guidance given to parents of deaf children during the last twenty years have been outstanding contributions to this field of education. It is now possible for children to enter school understanding a considerable number of words and phrases and having a useful vocabulary which can be pronounced in a more or less natural tone with clearly distinguishable vowels and a number of correctly articulated consonants. Not all children, unfortunately, receive such help and not all who do reach the standards described above. Present aims are to extend this provision as widely as possible and to make it possible for more children to achieve higher linguistic standards.

NURSERY CLASSES

With this greater facility in the use and understanding of language on the part of an increasing number of children entering school, the teacher at the nursery stage finds that linguistic development can proceed much more rapidly. Yet it is often noted that some children are apparently doing less well at the end of their first year at school than would have been expected from their attainments upon entry. It is possible that this lack of progress may result from a too abrupt transition from home to school. As the authors of *Periods of Stress in the Primary School* (6) point out, "starting school is for the child a second weaning process". They also go on to suggest that "from the point of view of the child, then, it is helpful when the school regime does not differ markedly from the regime at home, when home can be carried over into school, when strange experiences can be assimilated with the help of parents who know the teacher and the school and when it is already a familiar experience to be with other children of the same age". If this is one of the periods when a child with normal hearing is likely to undergo stress, how much more likely is it that a deaf child will experience even greater stress! Linguistic difficulties make the matter of communicating experiences and receiving reassurances much less satisfactory and satisfying. The resultant period of emotional strain may not show itself in overt behaviour but it may be just as real and significant as if it had done so. These stresses, together with the different environment and routine of the school, may cause temporary checks in the development of communication skills. Consequently, the guidance given to parents must help them to try to prepare children for school, whether it be day or boarding, and, of course, the greater the linguistic development before the child goes to school the easier will this preparation be. However, the nursery school has also an extremely important role to play in this adjustment process and it can do this best by ensuring that the gradient of change from home to school is as gentle as possible. The routine situations of home which were the mainsprings of communication, mealtimes, washing, going out for a walk, helping mother in the kitchen and about the house, should have their counterparts in the nursery class. Some of these can be real situations, others can be played out in a 'Wendy' house or corner of the classroom. At the same time there will be considerable periods of free play which are necessary not only in the same way that play is necessary for all young children and in order that the children may gradually mature from parallel to co-operative play, but also that the teacher may have an opportunity of joining in the free play of individual children and of using this time as a period for practising communication skills.

Although these children have been described as deaf, most of them will have some residual hearing. Less than 7 per cent of them will be totally deaf and probably not more than another 10 per cent will obtain only minimal benefits from amplification.* For the remainder a great deal of use can be made of their residual hearing but for the most part when it is used in conjunction with lipreading. Some children at the lower end (in terms of hearing loss) of this group may learn to distinguish some sounds, principally vowels, by hearing alone, but a hearing aid will be most effective, even for them, when they can look as well as listen. The information needed by the teacher, suitable arrangements and equipment, and some suggestions for methods of using it, have already been given in Chapter 4.

'Looking' involves lipreading and the comprehension of speech that may be achieved from watching the speaker's face. Since, as has already been pointed out, profoundly deaf children will not be able to discriminate speech accurately by hearing alone, and some indeed may get little more than the sound of voices through their aids, it is clear that 'looking' is an extremely important part of this two-channel method of speech comprehension. All severely and profoundly deaf children will need to rely on it to a very great extent and for many it will remain their main means of understanding. It is necessary to stress this point since, just as effective use may not be made of hearing aids, so efficiency in lipreading may be disregarded. To a considerable extent, the benefit from each of these communication channels is dependent not only upon the amount of residual hearing but also upon the nature of the early training which a child has received. A profoundly deaf child who has worn an aid from early infancy and whose parents have, under guidance, used it effectively, will make much more use of his hearing in later life than a child with a similar degree of hearing loss who has not had the opportunity

* These figures refer to the deaf children and not to the total population of schools for the deaf, of whose number about 40 per cent might be described as moderately or severely deaf. The other 60 per cent is the population to which these figures refer.

of listening to amplified speech until he comes to school. The former will be a 'listener' who uses lipreading to help him to understand: the latter will be a 'looker' who can hear something through an aid but never makes as much use of what he can hear. The child's early experiences in listening, or lack of them, should be well known to the teacher when he enters the nursery school so that she can base her approach on them.

In an educational approach which involves looking and listening, a teacher must be well aware of the necessity of helping children in both. Teacher and children must be well placed a regards light and a favourable distance for lipreading. Her speech patterns must be as easy as possible to lipread—clear, unexaggerated moderately paced and interesting to look at. The necessary contextual clues to help with meaning must also be given. At the same time, the children must be able to get as good patterns of speech as possible through their aids. This means speech close to the microphone by the teacher and also by the pupils, so that each hears his own voice and that of classmates as well as possible Optimum volume settings for each child must be known; the teacher must monitor the input of her voice and the children must be helped to do this. All this calls for a high degree of skill on the part of the teacher, but unless all these aspects are taken into account, the pupils will not receive the patterns of speech which will help them most nor will they be getting the 'feed-back necessary for the development of spoken language.

It was suggested above that, at the nursery stage, the main means of developing understanding and use of spoken language will be through activities which are not too far removed from the domestic situations with which the children are familiar. Even for those children who have had the benefit of pre-school training by their parents, these situations will still be very appropriate For these activities the use of an inductance loop system seems to be the most useful. The children are able to move about the room freely, wearing their individual aids, whilst the teacher speaking closely into the microphone, gives them as good patterns of speech as are possible through wearable aids with their frequency (and sometimes intensity) limitations. It should be remembered, however, that the children are not likely to hear the sound of their own voices or those of other pupils unless very powerful commercial aids are used, or they wear a second aid for this specific purpose.

As well as these informal activities and the formation of small groups engaged in similar activities directed by the teacher, a beginning is made at this stage of getting the whole class to come together for a story or a communal activity, such as opening a parcel, or creative work, such as finger painting, or rhythm work moving to music. These communal activities are at first voluntary, but when interest is skilfully aroused most, if not all, the children are prepared to join in. Here, by a combination of looking and listening, the teacher develops an understanding of spoken language in clear-cut situations and encourages the children to express themselves relevantly, at first perhaps only in single words, but as soon as possible helping them to put one or two words together. Time must be found by the teacher, usually when the children are engaged in free activities, to have a short period of individual speech with each child. Children who have had pre-school training should be at the stage of 'articulation readiness',* and much of the individual work at this point will consist in developing the concepts of 'using voice', 'flicking', 'making it louder (or softer)', 'smooth', 'at the front', 'at the back', etc. Even for profoundly deaf children it will also involve brief periods of listening practice when they try to identify, for example, one toy out of a group of three, the names of which contain different long vowels. Children who have not had pre-school training may need the opportunity to pass through the stage of 'speech readiness'† first of all, although this should not need to take a great deal of time at this stage of maturation.

Groht (7) has suggested that in a nursery school "the people in charge should be thoroughly trained nursery school teachers—not trained teachers of the deaf". It may be that in the United States it is not possible to be both, but in Britain it is fairly common to find that those in charge of nursery classes for deaf children are both fully-trained nursery teachers and trained teachers of the deaf. This seems to be essential if the children are to get the greatest benefit from attendance at a nursery school. It is only the trained teacher of the deaf who can help the children to attain the maximum development of spoken language through looking and listening. On the other hand, training as a nursery

---

* For a fuller description of this term see Ewing *Speech and the Deaf Child:* pp. 143-56.

† *ibid.*, pp. 131-42.

H

teacher is equally important in so far as the social development of the children is concerned. This aspect of nursery school work must take an important place in nursery classes for deaf children. It involves helping children to make friendly contact with other children and at the same time to develop self-reliance and independence. De Lissa (8) suggests that in a nursery school "the teacher must, by the atmosphere she creates and the general arrangements she introduces, devote herself to the task of making sociable and not unsociable acts enjoyable. Every child must be made to feel that he has a place, is loved and expected to be helpful to all".

INFANT CLASSES

The transition from nursery class to infant class is to a very large extent an imperceptible rather than an abrupt change. Gesell (9) considers that at five "the tides of development run smoothly". However, he reports that between the ages of five and six fundamental changes begin to take place. New traits, such as self-centredness, emotional tensions and outbursts, become apparent and there are physical changes resulting in increased susceptibility to infectious diseases. By the time the child has reached the age of seven and passed into the junior school many of these changes will have become stabilised. The significance of this is, however, that although the change from nursery class to infant class may be fairly smooth, there are physical and psychological changes taking place whilst a child is in the infant department that are part of the normal process of maturation. Teachers of deaf as well as of other children should be aware of these changes and be prepared, as far as possible, to meet them. Praise for effort seems to provide good motivation but activities need to be varied and not too lengthy. At this stage, too, the pupils are quite demanding and tend to want individual adult attention. Whilst meeting such needs as far as she is able, the teacher must also contribute towards social development by sharing her time equitably with the group.

The main aim in the infant classes should be to encourage and develop spoken language. Reading, as will be indicated later, is a skill that must be acquired but overdependence on reading or any other means of communication at this stage will reduce the need for and therefore progress in spoken language. The main object, for the greater part of the school day (and beyond it), must be to foster spoken language or talking on the part of the child. Unless a deaf pupil has acquired the habit of expressing himself in speech by the end of the infant stage, it is doubtful if he will ever make any real progress in oral work. This does not mean that a high degree of skill must be attained at this point, but it does mean that the habit must be well established. To achieve this constant practice is required and therefore 'language lessons' in the infant department, and many other lessons besides, must have as their main aim the encouragement of spoken language.

Dr Groht (7) in discussing how to teach new language suggests that "this should be done in a natural way, making full use of the child's interests, experiences and needs. It should never be done through the use of extraneous materials, drill sentences, or artificial exercises devoid of personal interest and entirely outside the child's need for the language being taught". At the infant stage, perhaps the two best techniques for developing language in this natural way are directed activities and story-telling. Activities at this stage and in this context are teacher-directed, but they are based on the interests of the children. The types of activity which seem to be popular are those involving the preparation of food and drinks—making orange drinks in the summer, hot drinks in the winter, a jelly, jam tarts, gingerbread boy, biscuits and the like; the imitation of domestic activities—washing-up, washing doll's clothes, planting bulbs and seeds in season; and simple handwork—making of articles for a model, houses, trees, etc., making puppets, making models from cardboard or weaving, etc.

Stories can, of course, be extremely varied. They may relate to simple activities with which the children are familiar, e.g. going shopping; simple dramatic stories of other children fishing, travelling and so forth; the doings of pets; and seasonal happenings. They may relate to less familiar situations and countries, e.g. activities of children in other lands, what happens to a letter when it is posted, fairy tales, or stories about animals. Whatever the topic of a story may be there is usually in common with others the fact that it, or parts of it, can be dramatised by the children—one of the surest ways by which it is possible to assess the children's comprehension of the story—or it can be illustrated by pictures or drawing.

As examples of the techniques of dealing with these two types of lessons the following may help to illustrate the ways in which spoken language may be developed. A directed activity might be selected which would involve washing-up utensils after a lesson in which something had been made. The children would be wearing individual hearing aids with an inductance loop system, the teacher wearing a collar microphone. The children would be seated in a semi-circle round or near the sink—an essential piece of classroom equipment. The lesson might begin somewhat as follows:

TEACHER: (*indicating the collection of dirty dishes*) What shall we do with the dirty dishes, the dirty plates, the dirty basin, the dirty spoons?

A child will probably volunteer the word 'wash'.

TEACHER: That's right. We shall wash them. Can you say wash them?

Child attempts to repeat this, the teacher giving a good pattern into the microphone.

TEACHER: Let us all say it: wash them.

Children all say it.

TEACHER: Listen. It's wa*sh* them. Can you say *sh*? Now listen, wa*sh*. All say it: wash them.

Children all say it.

TEACHER: What shall we do, Jean?

JEAN: Wash them.

TEACHER: What shall we do, John?

JOHN: Wash them.

TEACHER: What shall we do, Mary?

MARY: Wash them.

TEACHER: That's right. We shall wash the dirty dishes. Where shall we wash them?

Possibly the required word 'bowl' may be forthcoming from one child and if so the teacher gives the phrase 'in a bowl'. Several children are then encouraged to reply to the question 'Where shall we wash them?' by 'In a bowl'.

TEACHER: What do we need in the bowl?

It is likely that one child will volunteer the word 'water'.

TEACHER: Yes, we need water. What do we need, Michael? . . . James? . . . Mary?

Where necessary the pronunciation of the word 'water' will be improved without spending too much time on this.

TEACHER: Do we need hot water or cold water?

If the children do not grasp this question the teacher gets two bowls and

puts hot water in one and cold in the other. She holds up one bowl.
    What is this water?
Child is allowed to feel the water and it is likely he will reply 'hot'.
TEACHER: Yes, it is hot water. Say hot water, William, . . .
    Mary, . . . Robert. (*She holds up the other bowl.*) What is this
    water? (*Child feels the water and probably replies 'cold'.*)
TEACHER: Yes, it is cold water. Say 'cold water'.
*Teacher gets a few children to say this. Teacher then holds up bowl of
hot water and asks 'What is this?' A few children will be asked to
reply. Then she holds up the bowl of cold water and gets a few replies
to the question in the same way as before.*
TEACHER: (*returning to original question*) Do we need hot water or
    cold water to wash the dirty dishes?
This time she should get the reply 'hot water'.
TEACHER: Who can put some hot water in the bowl?
Pupils put their hands up and one is selected.
TEACHER: What are you going to do, Margaret?
MARGARET: Hot water.
TEACHER: Where will you put the hot water
MARAGRET: Bowl. *or* In the bowl.
TEACHER: Yes. Put hot water in the bowl. Say it all, Margaret
    (*holding microphone close to her mouth*).
TEACHER: Yes, Margaret. Put hot water in the bowl.
Margaret puts some hot water in the bowl and teacher turns to the class.
TEACHER: What did Margaret do? (*There are probably some
    incomplete replies from the children.*) Margaret, come and tell
    the others what you did.
MARGARET: Put hot water in the bowl.
TEACHER: (*again to class*) What did Margaret do?
*Teacher builds up replies from the pupils into the sentence and gives
most members of the class the opportunity of saying the sentence. She
holds the microphone close to their mouths whilst they reply, the other
pupils being required to look and listen to the child who is speaking.*

The lesson will continue in much the same pattern—getting the
children to think what the answer will be, making it into a
reasonably correct phrase or sentence and then practising it.
Perhaps enough has been indicated to make the pattern clear.
The main points are as much talking as possible by the children,
the clear-cut context and the encouragement to use simple phrases
and sentences wherever they are appropriate. If there are new

words these should be written on a side blackboard and later copied by the children into their own notebook dictionaries.

It will also be apparent that although the lesson looks longer in print than it is in actual fact, the pace is nevertheless slow. This is inevitable at this stage if all the pupils are to be expected to make contributions in reasonably correct English. It does, however, point to the fact that these activities should be fairly brief so that interest can be maintained for the whole of the lesson. With an experienced teacher such a lesson might go on for thirty minutes, but usually twenty minutes is sufficiently long. It is much better at this stage to have fairly short periods and keep the interest at a high level than let the lesson drag on. As the children become more experienced in this pattern of lesson and as their ability to put words together improves, the pace of lessons will speed up and more ground can be covered.

The pattern which has been outlined above should be the basic pattern for a directed activity of the kind suggested above. The same pattern should not be repeated too frequently and a skilful teacher will think out ways of varying it, giving the necessary repetition practice in vocabulary and sentence construction, whilst retaining the essential principles upon which this type of lesson is based.

The main ingredients of a story are not so very different from those of an activity. The main aims are again to get the children to comprehend by looking and listening, to think and express their ideas in words and to ensure that they have understood by checking their understanding at all points and in as great a variety of ways as possible. With an infant class wearing individual aids with an inductance loop system, such a lesson might begin as follows:

TEACHER: One day a little boy called Jim went for a walk with his dog.

What was the little boy's name?

Who will be Jim? All right, Tony, you be Jim.

Now, who went with Jim?

Who will be the dog? All right, Mary, you be the dog.

One day a little boy called Jim went for a walk with his dog.

Jim and the dog, go for a walk.

When this has been grasped teacher produces a drawing of a boy and his dog going for a walk. This is shown to the class and then placed on a ledge or fastened to the blackboard.

TEACHER: They saw a little boy playing with a ball.
> Who will be the little boy? All right, Fred, you are the little
> boy.
> What was the little boy playing with? Yes, a ball. Who can
> find a ball?
> They saw a little boy playing with a ball.
> Little boy, play with the ball.

When is it evident that this sentence has been clearly understood a second appropriate illustration is produced.

TEACHER: The ball rolled into a river.
> Show me a river. (Children indicate picture of a river on a
> wall-chart, or draw a river in chalk on the floor.)
> Who can roll the ball into the river? No, that is not 'rolled',
> that is 'bounced'. Who can show me 'rolled'? (If necessary
> the teacher may have to demonstrate this.)
> Now, show me 'the ball rolled into the river'.

When this has been done a third illustration is shown.

The story will continue for three or more sentences. At the
end of the story when there might have been six or seven illustrations of each event in the story, the teacher might check further
the children's ability to comprehend sentences by asking the
following questions:

> Who can show me the picture of the ball rolling into the river?
> Who can show me the picture of Jim and his dog going for a
> walk?
> Who can show me the picture of the little boy playing with a
> ball?

This story is, of course, at a very simple level and does not
demand much more than comprehension. As children become
more experienced they will be asked to think out the probable
next step in the story—where did they go for a walk? When this
stage has been reached it will no longer be necessary to dramatise
the parts of the story since the suggestions made by the children
will themselves indicate how far the children have comprehended
the preceding sentence.

Other ways in which spoken language should be developed
at this stage relate to the incidents which have happened at home
or outside school and which the children wish to communicate
to the teacher. Frequently, the children's abilities to 'get across'
their ideas to the teacher are very much less well developed than

the ideas themselves and their desire to communicate them. One way of helping to overcome this difficulty is by the institution of a home/school notebook. Such a notebook would be applicable either to the situation when children attend school as day pupils or when they remain at school as weekly boarders and return home for the week-end. In this notebook, the parent records briefly some of the events of the evening or the week-end, e.g. "played with his cars before tea, after tea watched . . . on TV" or "on Saturday went shopping with me in the morning, played on his tricycle with the girl next door in the afternoon". The return entry from school might be "learned to give a good initial 'k' sound. When he next plays with his cars, make sure he uses it". Such a book is not only helpful to the teacher in seeking to develop language, but it makes the parents feel that they can help with their child's education and assist in the growth of their understanding of their child's problems.

At the infant stage, a beginning will be made with reading and written language. The imperfect patterns of words which are received through lipreading or aided hearing make the need for the more complete and permanent written form even more essential for deaf than hearing children. It also underlies the earlier beginning with reading that is found in schools for the deaf. Whilst the early introduction of reading for deaf children is essential on these grounds, it must be reiterated that communication should be mainly by oral means if oral fluency is to be achieved. This follows the normal pattern of development in which a hearing child has been talking for at least three years before he is introduced to reading. Learning to read and learning to write after the acquisition of a considerable spoken and understood vocabulary then become special skills to be developed rather than the main medium through which the mother tongue has to be learned. Conversely, one of the basic causes of backwardness in reading is deficiency in language.

The principles of teaching reading to deaf children are, in the main, the same as those on which the teaching of reading to hearing children are based. "The first step to literacy is through speech", states a Ministry of Education pamphlet on reading (10), and the apophthegm is echoed by numerous writers on the subject. Schonell, for example, states that "saying and hearing words are the essential factor in their later recognition", and "learning to read must be preceded and accompanied by a background of language experiences obtained through home and school" (11). Whilst recognising the paucity of a deaf child's language experiences in comparison with those of a hearing child, the principle is nevertheless still relevant: that the more extensive the comprehended and spoken vocabulary of a deaf child the easier it is for him to make a good start with reading.

Pre-reading activities, such as matching, whilst important in training children to perceive small differences and therefore in leading towards recognition of differences in words, are perhaps less fundamental in their importance than the acquisition of a good vocabulary, both words which are understood and words to be spoken. These activities will certainly be of help in the development of reading but by themselves will not make children able to read. When children have acquired a fair-sized vocabulary (say, of approximately one hundred words understood and thirty words spoken) the written pattern should be introduced and a beginning made with reading. This means that something approximating to the 'look and say' method should be used. Whenever possible, however, the words should be used and written in short phrases or sentences so that the children can relate them to lipreading patterns (which are seldom, if ever, single words) and the patterns of spoken English which they are being encouraged to use. Thus, although it may be necessary to draw attention to a particular word, instead of the common practice of labelling objects in the classroom with their names, it is better to label them with a short descriptive sentence. Thus, instead of 'the table', 'the window', 'a chair', 'a leg', the following captions on labels in the appropriate places might be used: 'The table has four legs'; 'The window is made of glass'; 'The chair has four legs'; 'The chair has a back', etc. Other ways of helping the children to relate short sentences or phrases to meaningful experiences is by labelling of children's drawings and paintings by the teacher with the phrase or sentence given by the child (and probably corrected) when asked what the picture is about. In the early stages, reading for deaf, as for hearing, children should be closely linked with meaningful experiences. It should consist in learning to interpret the written symbols of words which the child understands and uses. Unless a child learns to do just this, reading for him is not a means of understanding the thought or ideas conveyed by the symbols but simply a barren exercise.

Since reading and writing are complementary, the latter should begin at the same time as the former. If the teacher has labelled a drawing the child can go over the writing with a coloured crayon. When he can do this he is generally able to copy a short phrase from a pattern given by the teacher. Of course, practice must be given in forming the letters correctly and some help in acquiring this skill is obtained through 'writing' with the finger in the air or on the desk. The kinaesthetic sensations thus obtained help to develop motor control. Actual practice in writing the letters, though formal, is an experience enjoyed by most children and seems to be one which is necessary in order to achieve success through a simple trial and error process.

Whilst most teachers of deaf children would willingly sacrifice accuracy in speech for spontaneity, none the less, even at this stage, the achievement of greater accuracy in pronunciation must be aimed at, otherwise bad habits are established which become more and more difficult to eradicate as time goes on. There used to be some controversy about the extent to which 'approximate speech' should be accepted. Any heat generated by this has long since vanished and the simple answer to the question would seem to be that all spoken contributions should be welcomed but that the best speech of which a child is capable at that stage should be expected and encouraged. In addition, of course, much more positive steps must be taken to improve speech at this stage. Whilst some of these steps can be taken with the whole class as a group, most of the practice must be given on an individual, or very small group, basis. It is therefore important for the infant teacher to arrange that each child should have at least one short period of individual speech practice each day. This is a minimum requirement and it is an essential one. The speech of deaf children will not improve unless positive and systematic steps are taken to ensure that this carefully directed practice takes place each day and, if possible, for more than one short period. The teacher of an infant class consisting of ten pupils who has no other adult help will certainly find it no easy task to make the appropriate arrangements. This problem adds substance to the proposal that classes should be reduced in size to not more than eight and preferably six pupils. However, even the teacher with eight or more pupils must still make some appropriate arrangements. If it is not possible to take a child aside for a five-minute period of practice whilst the other children are engaged in an activity which does not require the teacher's attention, then some system of combining two classes for short periods is another possible solution. In this case one of the teachers is responsible for her own and her colleague's class for a certain activity whilst the colleague takes pupils individually for short periods of speech practice. The provision of untrained helpers in infant classes is another system which enables the class teacher to have time for individual work in speech and other subjects. Yet another solution, adopted in some other countries, is that of providing the services of teachers who have no class responsibility but take special responsibility as speech specialists. On the whole, most teachers in Britain seem to dislike this plan since they do not know precisely what has been done and achieved in this special lesson nor do they have the opportunity of undertaking personally what, for many teachers, is the most exciting and fascinating part of their work.

Reference was made, when discussing the nursery stage, to articulation readiness. Some children will not have reached this stage before the infant level and all the pupils at this level will need further practice in helping them to develop speech sounds. The techniques suggested by the late Lady Ewing (12) for helping to develop speech sounds are most strongly recommended as leading to highly successful results when followed systematically and intelligently, They involve learning by 'insight' rather than by 'trial and error', are psychologically soundly based and can sustain the child's interest when applied sensibly. The approach is a multi-sensory one which includes capitalising on whatever residual hearing a child may have in addition to visual, tactile and kin-aesthetic sensations that may be perceived. This means that during individual speech lessons a speech training aid should be used to give a pupil the maximum opportunity of hearing his own voice and matching the patterns with those of the teacher than can be perceived. This demands knowledge, on the part of the teacher, of the child's hearing capacity, the characteristics of the speech sounds being used, and the physical characteristics of the hearing aid itself. Where it is clear that for one reason or another a child cannot hear a sound, then the other senses are brought into play to assist. Even when hearing is possible, the auditory pattern very often needs to be linked with the tactile, kinaesthetic and visual pattern so that each modality will reinforce the other, give a greater wholeness to the pattern and give the child as wide a range of clues as possible for repetition and recall. Not only should the pronunciation of sounds, vowel and consonant, be improved and, where possible, thoroughly learned, but practice at this stage should be given in trying to obtain variations in intonation and rhythm. The use of pitch indicators and any other means of giving visual clues to assist the imperfect auditory ones is found to be very valuable for this purpose. Reference has already been made to the importance of a child being enabled to hear his own spoken patterns: speech close to the microphone by the child as well as by the teacher is the best means of promoting this and the significance of this cybernetic approach has been stressed by a number of writers, especially those working in the Netherlands (13).

The above remarks on speech development and improvement have related mainly to special periods of speech work. Neither the teacher nor the pupils should, however, be under the impression that this is the only time that speech matters. 'Incidental' speech improvement must be carried on in every lesson that involves speech by the pupils. Whenever a new word is introduced into a lesson the teacher must ensure that the class members are each given an opportunity to say it. The teacher will give some help first by, for example, indicating the number of syllables, showing which syllable is stressed, indicating the pronunciation of particular phonemes ('k' for the written 'c' at the beginning of 'car') and then giving a good auditory and visual pattern for the pupils to copy. As well as dealing with new words in this way most children will need to be reminded about the correct phoneme in words which are already familiar and perhaps asked to repeat their statement, thinking more carefully about the pronunciation of certain sounds.

Before concluding this brief review of education at the infant stage, a few points need to be made about other subjects that are generally included in the curriculum. One of these is the development of number work. At the infant stage, a great deal of this will consist of preparatory experiences. These will include pouring water into containers of different shapes and capacity; weighing of objects; simple 'shopping'; and counting. In addition to learning to count, which, of course, means that the child has to learn the number names in the proper sequence, it is necessary for him to recognise number groups and relate these to number symbols. For the development of notation, one or two systems using special structural equipment, such as rods or blocks, have been introduced comparatively recently. The best known of these systems are the Cuisenaire, the Stern, Colour Factor and the Multibase Arithmetic Blocks. The first named is perhaps the best known in this country and a number of schools and local authorities have adopted it and appear to be enthusiastic about the results which have followed from its introduction. Some schools for the deaf have also used it with considerable success. Too early a start should not be made with formal 'sums': number work can be included in a variety of activities at this stage and, until the children are familiar with number names, number sequence and can readily recognise number groups, there is no advantage to be gained by proceeding to abstractions. It is also helpful at this stage to begin to introduce certain number concepts in relation to the appropriate language forms. Such concepts will include more, less, one more, heavy, light, long, short, a lot of, a little, and others. These are best developed through activities and stories.

Other subjects, such as handwork, art, physical education and games are included in the curriculum at this stage. By referring to them as subjects, however, they immediately become formalised and assume an independent status. The school day in the infant class should primarily be spent in a succession of activities and experiences. Some of these will be oriented in one direction, some in another, and in most there will be a variety of experiences which are providing the bases for 'subjects' such as reading, number, English, and so forth. It should perhaps here be stressed that the activities and arrangements in an infant class for deaf children should not differ markedly from the arrangements for similar classes for hearing pupils. The group work, noted above, will only occupy a part of the school day and the provision of materials for free play and other activities should be similar to that for hearing children at the same stage. It is extremely important, yet far from easy, for the teacher to encourage as much vocalisation as possible, and preferably the use of words and phrases that have been learned, not only in the children's communication with her but in their communication with each other during the activities.

Fundamental to everything is the encouragement of the maximum of spoken language, whatever the activity. Teaching a deaf child to use the appropriate words in different kinds of activity and to express the ideas evoked by these various activities is the greatest contribution that can be made to his overall development at this stage.

JUNIOR STAGE

"Young children are active, curious, talkative and energetic and education should satisfy those needs and provide opportunities for their expression in forms that will help the child's growth towards maturity" (14). This succint summary of the characteristics of junior school pupils and the principles on which the curriculum should be based is a good example of modern attitudes to education in the primary school. A variety of books with such titles as *Activity in the Primary School, Purpose in the Junior School,* and *Exploration in the Junior School* reflect the same attitude which was summarised by the Consultative Committee in the Report on the Primary School (1931) when they suggested that the curriculum was to be "thought of in terms of activity and experience rather than of knowledge to be acquired and facts to be stored" (15). Inasmuch as deaf children are primarily children, the same principles are relevant in their education at this stage. It is true that their handicap with its attendant problems of linguistic development will have a profound bearing on methods of teaching, yet this should not absolve us from recognising that the curriculum must be based on activities and experiences.

Linguistic Development

As at the infant stage, and indeed at all stages of schooling, the main aims will be related to developing language as a means of thinking and as a vehicle for the communication of ideas. The thoughts, however, will be about the interesting experiences with which the child is familiar and the subjects which interest a child at his level of maturity; communication will be encouraged when there is purpose in gaining and giving information.

It is usual practice at this stage for pupils to be working together as a class for a considerable part of the school day, and for the teacher to give what are described as 'class lessons'. It is arguable that, in view of what has previously been said about the lack of homogeneity in the composition of most classes, these class lessons should be much more limited in number and more use should be made of smaller groups as learning units. The teacher must carefully decide which parts of the curriculum are appropriate for class lessons and which are only suitable for smaller groups, if learning is to be effective. These smaller groups would probably change their composition for different activities since it does not follow that children who are at the same stage in reading will necessarily be at the same stage in number work or be able to deal with a new experience in the same way. On the whole, there is much to be said in favour of breaking the class into smaller units whose number and composition will vary according to the activity. Such smaller groups give the teacher the opportunity to concentrate on the particular and common needs of a small group; give more opportunities for individual spoken expression; and give the children who are working on other tasks, whilst the teacher is busy with one group, the practice they need in learning to work independently without continuous adult support and with some responsibility for their own learning. Practices of this kind in some junior schools can provide teachers of the deaf with examples of the ways in which children learn in small groups. But here, as at the infant stage, it is important that the children should learn to communicate with each other during these small group activities by means of spoken language. Ways in which this might be facilitated are dealt with in Chapter 4.

If, as seems possible within the next decade, some use will be made in schools for the deaf of programmed learning, probably involving 'teaching machines', this group work will facilitate such arrangements and made the transfer to this type of learning quite simple. Each of the smaller groups in turn would be able to undertake individual work of this type whilst the teacher worked with another group.

Whether class or group work is undertaken there is a strong case at the junior stage for the provision of a group hearing aid within each classroom. Such an aid will give the class or smaller groups the opportunity of hearing the teacher's voice close to the microphone, of each child hearing both his own and the other pupils' voices speaking close to a microphone and of getting, through the telephones, speech patterns which are the best possible in terms of intensity and frequency. Group aids are, of course, somewhat limiting in terms of movement on the part of the pupils around the classroom, but there are enough occasions during the day, even with a curriculum which is oriented towards 'activity', when the children should be sitting in their places talking and listening. For these periods the group aid provides the optimum auditory experience although, as has already been pointed out, this auditory experience must be supplemented by looking, or lipreading, and this must be taken into account in the seating arrangements.

For children who can benefit from the use of wearable aids, these should be provided for occasions when the use of a group aid is inappropriate. Within the classroom the individual aids will usually be used in conjunction with an inductance loop system. The settings of the aids (as of the group aid) should be determined in the manner described in Chapter 3.

In the lower classes of the junior school much of the language development can take place through a continuation of the technique of 'directed activities' as described for the infant classes. This would be in line with the philosophy outlined at the beginning of this section and it would provide the motivation for communication. The kind of activities would, of course, be those which were suited to the ages of the pupils and their interests. The beginnings of simple nature study and science, road safety, learning to do everyday jobs and making of a variety of models, are examples of the kind of activities that could be treated in this way. The teacher's task is to get the children to understand, through looking and listening, what she is telling them or asking them to do; to communicate their ideas through speech and to describe what is being done. In terms of understanding this will mean that practice will be given in developing the children's span of attention so that they can comprehend several ideas expressed in one or two sentences. It will also mean giving the children the opportunity to think about what should be done (What shall we do next?) and then of expressing these ideas in spoken language. With some children it may be necessary at the beginning of the junior stage to accept answers of only one or two words, but as quickly as possible these should be developed into phrases and short sentences. As far as possible idiomatic English should be taught and the children given the opportunity to practise it. A skilful teacher will arrange for frequent repetition of the same sentence pattern in a lesson so that the children can have the opportunity, on the one hand, of seeing and hearing the pattern repeated and, on the other, of using the pattern themselves when they talk. This repetition of sentence patterns in varying contexts and, of course, without using identical vocabulary each time, is the best way of ensuring that these patterns become fixed without resorting to repetitive drill methods which have little meaning for the pupils and which cannot be related by them to their proper context. It is through such practices that pronouns, prepositions and the comprehension and use of question forms such as Who? and What? and How many? can be most appropriately learned. Again, with skilfully arranged repetition, it is possible to give the children a great deal of practice, without formal drilling, in these language forms.

In addition to these activities in the classroom, much language teaching can be based on what could be described as environmental studies. The aim of such studies is to get the children to observe, talk and write about the environment of the school and what goes on there. These studies will involve geography, nature study and some history (especially with the older classes). Children will learn to draw maps, discover what kind of buildings are in the area and their use, find out what kind of work is carried out, and observe the plant, animal and bird life. Not only is this enrichment of experience part of the general education of children, but it provides interesting experiences around which language may be built. These activities are often best carried out on a group basis with two or three children co-operating in one aspect of the activity. For example, if the particular study being made is the natural history of a park or other area, one group might be asked to find out the different trees, another to look for plants, a third to see how many species of birds can be found and a fourth to look for insects. As well as this horizontal study, a vertical study of the area at different seasons of the year could be made. The material is talked about, written about, drawings are made and all probably incorporated into a class book on the subject.

The third main area on which language teaching can be based is covered by the more traditional class lessons on such subjects as life and work in other lands and stories of the past. In these lessons much more direct teaching is done by the teacher, but as well as providing opportunities for developing comprehension on the part of the pupils through looking and listening, they can help in developing the pupils' thinking and reasoning, in terms of comparisons and reasons for differences, and the enlargement of vocabulary. They can also serve to encourage children to consult books to find out information.

Some schools make use of 'centres of interest' to provide the basis for much of the learning that goes on. This way of organising

I

the curriculum round a specific topic has much to commend it, although it carries with it the risk of trying to find somewhat tenuous connections between the different heads or sub-topics into which the main centre of interest is divided. Basically, however, the principle is sound and the division of the curriculum into watertight compartments, each labelled with a subject name, is neither particularly relevant to the needs of the children nor desirable in view of the fact that much of the process of learning is the perception of relationships. W. D. Wall, writing about the primary school (16) states that "at this early stage other know-ledge, in the sense of an ordered and coherent body of facts called botany, biology, history, geography, grammar or the like, has little relevance in and for itself". He goes on to say: "Certainly education . . . cannot be without content. But the importance of facts in the primary school years lies more in the stimulus which they give to particular modes of thinking, the raw material their interrelationships give for the child's developing ability to conceptualize, to think and to express, than to their place in a systematic adult construct."

All these ways, described above, of developing language have a solid psychological basis. They meet the needs of children at this stage, they provide interest and they can help to develop concepts based on language and thinking in words. As at the infant stage, the spoken expression of the pupils is the most important aspect of language development and at all times the course of the lesson or activity should be directed to obtain as much spoken language from the pupils as possible. A further principle that needs to be applied in the use of spoken language is that of self-correction. The pupils at this stage must learn to begin to take responsibility for improving their expression. Incorrect expressions should not immediately be corrected by the teacher; the pupil should learn to react positively to phrases such as "Now think! Now you can say that better! Think, and say that again."

Speech Improvement

Whilst emphasis has been laid on acquiring fluency in spoken language, it is essential that much time should be given at the junior stage to the improvement of speech. In discussing the needs of nursery and infant pupils, reference was made to the necessity for daily individual practice. This is still just as essential at the junior stage and, as before, is best carried out through the medium of a speech training aid. One of the essentials for a good teacher of speech is a critical ear. The teacher needs to listen carefully, occasionally with her eyes closed, so that she can analyse the speech of her pupils. This analysis will take account of voice quality and strength, the accuracy of pronunciation of vowels and consonants, the rate of utterance, the presence or absence of stress and rhythm and variations in pitch or intonation patterns. It will also try to assess the degree of intelligibility of the total speech pattern. A notebook should be kept for each child where such an analysis is entered and where a record is kept of work done and of achievements. A recording on magnetic tape should also be made, partly as an aid to the teacher in diagnosis and partly as a record for the future. These recordings should be made as often as seems necessary to help the teacher but at least an annual sample of speech should be kept on record. Where intelligibility does not seem to improve greatly over the year, the teacher will have to ask herself why this is so and what steps should be taken to bring about an improvement.

The main purpose of the analysis of a child's speech is to indicate on what lines an attack should be made in bringing about an improvement in naturalness and intelligibility. Ways in which vowel and consonant sounds as well as the other aspects of intelligible speech may be improved are set out in detail in *Speech and the Deaf Child* (12) and need not be further described here. Perhaps it should be reiterated, however, that whenever possible phonemes should be improved within the word setting by hearing and lipreading since this is the quickest and simplest way. When this does not bring about improvement either because the child cannot hear or see the phoneme or is unable to make the necessary adjustments of the speech organs, it may have to be taught in isolation and, once this has been done, put into a syllable and then a word for practice. Practice should be given in saying the phoneme in different words and in different positions in words so that mastery is achieved as soon as possible. Most deaf children find their greatest difficulty in pronouncing double and triple consonant groups and it may be comforting to a teacher of the deaf to remember that hearing children are frequently by no means secure in these until they are about eight years old. Care must be taken when pronouncing sounds either individually or in words that they are not drawled or prolonged.

An examination of five sentences spoken by seventeen severely deaf children revealed that they took an average time of 21·9 seconds to say them in comparison with the 13·5 seconds taken by hearing children. Drawled sounds and therefore drawn-out words contribute very significantly to loss of intelligibility and they are frequently the result of drawled patterns being used by the teacher in the teaching of phonemes. As with the content of spoken expression so with the pronunciation the pupil should gradually be helped to take responsibility for making his own best effort. When a pupil says something rather badly he should, certainly by the end of the junior stage if not earlier, be able to give a better version when the teacher suggests that he should. A phrase such as "Come, you can say that better" should be all that is required to effect this.

A method, described as the Hearing-Reading-Speaking Method and developed by Lady Ewing, is an extremely valuable means of developing fluency when a child has reached the stage of being able to read the words within his spoken vocabulary. Essentially the method involves the child listening to the spoken pattern of the teacher whilst she reads and points to a written (or printed) sentence. The child then repeats the sentence whilst the teacher again points to the written pattern. The reading by the teacher is carried out at normal speed and with normal phrasing and stress. Whilst the child is reading the pointing is done at the same speed and with the same rhythmic patterns. Several sentences are tackled in this way in the course of an individual lesson.

It seems to be generally true that the standard of speech achieved by a deaf pupil at the end of the junior stage will determine the standard he finally reaches on leaving school. By the age of eleven, and often before this, habits have been established which are not readily altered in the secondary stage. Improvement, of course, can and should come about at this later stage, but unless a pupil is using spoken langage fairly fluently and intelligibly by the end of the junior stage, it is unlikely that he will ever be an intelligible and fluent speaker. His syntactical patterns will develop and his vocabulary will increase at the secondary stage but it is only exceptionally that the quality of his speech will be better. This surely points to the very great importance of achieving as high a standard as possible at the junior stage.

Much has been said and written in recent years about the

advantages of auditory training. Whilst the present writer believes in the continuous use of hearing aids for all profoundly deaf children who can demonstrate that they can perceive any sound in this way, and has described how hearing aids should be used for different age-levels and types of lessons, it is not his belief that much time should be spent trying to teach profoundly deaf children to discriminate sounds of speech by hearing alone. At the beginning of this chapter the hearing loss of profoundly deaf pupils was defined as being in excess of 70 db for the frequencies 500 to 4,000 c.p.s. and, so far, few children with losses of this order have shown that they are able to discriminate much by hearing alone. Despite this, however, there is a very good case for helping these pupils to become aware of sounds, particularly of relating some everyday sounds to their source, and of becoming more attentive to the sounds they can hear. When possible, therefore, the teacher should try to weave into stories the sounds that might be appropriate. When the correct sounds cannot be produced in the classroom, a tape recorder plugged into the amplifier of the group aid can be used to reproduce the appropriate sound as the story is unfolded—the motor car engine, the dog barking, the cow mooing, and the sound of chopping wood, to suggest but a few examples. To give practice in attending closely to sounds various games can be played such as distinguishing monosyllables from disyllables and polysyllables, or telling which of four or five sentences written on the blackboard has been spoken. The aim in such games is to encourage the pupils to listen to the number of syllables or the rhythm of the phrase or sentence and not to expect phonemic discrimination. These games may be played as part of the group lesson or may be used for a few minutes during an individual speech lesson.

Some extremely valuable work in training profoundly deaf girls to perceive and interpret music has been carried out at St Michielsgestel in Holland. This training involves 'vibration feeling' as well as hearing and is applied to speech development as well as ballet. It is not possible to deal here adequately with the details of the methods used.

Reading

At the junior stage there is also a need to develop the skills of reading and writing. After spoken expression, reading is certainly the most important skill that should be developed. Many, if not most, deaf children seem to get off to a good start in reading at the infant stage. They pass through all the stages of readiness such as matching, putting picture sequences in correct order, labelling with the correct words, word recognition and so forth. However, after this start has been made the rate of development soon seems to slow down and many deaf children become retarded in reading. This slowness in the rate of progress compared with that of hearing children continues during the primary years until by the time children reach the age for secondary education they are retarded in reading. Brereton (17) in her study found that twelve-year-old children with hearing losses of around 57 db were often only able to cope with material understood by normal hearing children of the age of seven. Myklebust (18) found that deaf children did not reach the nine-year-old level of reading until they were sixteen or seventeen.

This retardation is not only a source of grave concern to many teachers but it is a matter of perplexity since 'reading for comprehension' is a silent process. Not all deaf children, of course, show a retardation as great as this and in some schools where there is a systematic reading programme in existence the gap is very much less than those quoted above. Children who are best at reading seem to be those who have a wide understood and spoken vocabulary. But it is not only the extent of the vocabulary that is important: it is essential to have a very broad concept of the meaning of the word that has to be read. Thus, for example, a child may know the word 'home' in the limited concept of the house where he lives, but more generalised ideas need to be taught and the word taught and used in a variety of contexts before the child begins to grasp the idea or concept of 'home'. Much of this is, of course, a maturing process but unless efforts are made by the teacher to help the children to generalise from the specific and to widen their concepts, the ideas for which words stand will be very limited. This is true not only with regard to vocabulary but also to the meaning of phrases. The child who interprets a phrase by the literal interpretation of each word without recognising interrelationships and the modifications that 'parts of speech' such as prepositions and adverbs may have on the ideas conveyed may well have a complete misconception of the meaning intended. For example, a word-by-word interpretation of the phrase 'to go home with James' may mean to the child that he is to go to his own home accompanied by James. Whilst this could be a correct interpretation, an equally normal valid usage, and perhaps the intention of the writer, would indicate that the child is going to James's home with him. English is, perhaps, a language where confusion may be greater than in many other European languages because of ambiguities in agreement of verb and subject and adjective and noun, but this does not resolve the problem for English-speaking children.

The development of reading skill, therefore, is not only a matter of increasing ability in word recognition and a widening of vocabulary, although these are, of course, involved. It is essentially associated with a development in verbal thinking. Miss Hart, whose book *Teaching Reading to Deaf Children* (19) is a very helpful text, states that "a well-balanced reading programme should include: adequate motivation, provision for evaluation, a wide variety of rich materials and a well-organised sequence of reading experiences". The provision of special reading books for deaf children, although helpful in many ways, is not the only way by which skill in reading may be improved. Such books provide suitable material for certain stages in reading ability, but these stages must be developed by the teacher through the encouragement of verbal thinking and reasoning. This can be done, as has been noted above, by the provision of interesting and meaningful experiences and then teaching the children the language patterns they need to talk and write about these experiences. This seems to be the fundamental approach to the improvement of reading in deaf children. There are ways in which specific aspects of reading skill may be improved. A number of books provide suggestions for games and exercises for improving word recognition, for increasing speed and for testing accuracy. One that the writer has found very helpful is published by Teachers' College, Columbia University (20). As a means of developing the ability to read unfamiliar words as they appear in a reader it seems to be useful at the junior stage to introduce a phonic system into reading. This helps the child to make an attempt at pronouncing the word and through pronunciation he should be able to recognise it as a word that he can say and that he has seen/heard before through lipreading/hearing.

It seems hardly necessary to stress the importance to deaf children of a high degree of skill in reading. The written pattern is not only more permanent but it is more complete than the pattern that can be obtained either through lipreading or aided hearing or a combination of both.

The provision of a class library is a valuable stimulus to interest in reading. The content should not be too static but should include some books relevant to topical interests as well as some of a more general appeal. At the junior stage pupils should be taught how to find specific pieces of information from reference and other books. This will mean that they need to be taught how to begin to use the school library as well as the class library. Such a library will obviously have a good selection of books suitable for different stages of reading skill and different interests. Books should be attractively set out and attempts made to have occasional special displays. Some suitable magazines (dealing with sports, hobbies, leisure-time pursuits and the like) for the older children should also be available.

Pupils should be made familiar with classification arrangements, beginning in a simple way in the junior school with knowing the shelves on which particular kinds of books may be found and leading on in the senior school to an ability to find books from a subject or author catalogue. Chairs and tables should be provided for the members of at least one class to use the library as a reading or study room.

Even in the junior school there should be a time, perhaps one period per week, when the children may sit in the library and examine and read the books that take their fancy. At the secondary stage library periods should serve a variety of functions—looking up information as part of the preparation of lessons; reading for pleasure; or studying books prescribed by the teacher. Usually, county libraries are very willing to loan sets of books to school libraries so that there is little excuse for the material in the library remaining static. The library can also be used by teachers with specialised interests to house displays and the finished products of projects or models that have been produced by their classes.

Written Expression

Writing, or written expression, generally accompanies reading. As a child learns to read a new word he is frequently given the opportunity of writing it, and simple sentence patterns which are familiar either through stories or 'news' are often written by the pupils. Written expression, however, means more than the ability to put down on paper familiar words or sentences. It involves the ability to write down one's ideas. Before it is possible to do this a child must be able to formulate these ideas in a conventional linguistic pattern. It would therefore seem that the best basis for written expression is oral expression. In a discussion of written expression, the authors of *The Primary School in Scotland* (21) suggest that most pupils will be unable to undertake this until they have passed out of the infant classes. In the latter, the pupils should be encouraged to develop 'oral expression'. Even at the beginning of the junior stage further practice in oral expression is required as a transition to written composition. If, as the authors of the report believe, children with normal hearing need more than two years' practice in oral expression after entering school, it seems likely that deaf children will need no less than this and very probably much more. Consequently, a great deal of practice in oral expression should be given to deaf children before they are expected to communicate their ideas in writing. The writing of words and short sentences at an earlier stage is important for the purpose of clarifying the symbols in the minds of the children, but the construction of a series of written sentences without adequate oral preparation will result in a meaningless repetition of the same hackneyed phrases which do not convey the ideas of the pupils. Most teachers will be familiar with written work which contains 'ideas' such as "Today is Tuesday. It was raining yesterday. We will go home on Friday." There is possibly a place for these at some stage of development but unless it is very quickly outgrown it will only serve to illustrate the paucity of a child's thinking in words.

An occasional 'news' period can be useful in helping to develop written expression, but the ideas need to come from the pupils and, where necessary, be put into correct English usage by the teacher. When the child can say the correct sentences he can then be given the opportunity to write them. This is one of the situations in which the use of a 'home/school notebook' through which the parents and teacher communicate with each other can be very valuable. Brief notes by the parents about what was done at home will help the teacher to elucidate some of the ideas which the pupils wish to communicate and enable her to help them build up the correct sentence patterns. In the lower junior classes, therefore, written expression should first of all be based on oral expression and should consist of sentences describing what the child did at home or at school, or what the child has observed during a lesson that has involved some activity on his part or a series of pictures used by the teacher to illustrate the main points of a story she has told to the class. In the upper junior classes the children need to be taught how to improve their written sentence patterns through the use of conjunctions or descriptive adjectives or adverbs. Letter writing is the most common form of composition needed in everyday life, and practice in this, beginning again with oral practice, should be given in the upper junior classes.

Practice must be given in the comprehenson of written material and in writing correct sentence patterns. Pugh, in an article entitled *Developing the Deaf Child's Power of Reasoning* (22) gives some very useful ideas for exercises of this kind. However, some consideration should also be given as to whether or not it would be helpful to use a more structured approach to language teaching which would give the pupils at least a temporary 'prop' in their learning of conventional word order. Such a technique need not detract from the principle enunciated above that language should be developed from experiences and interests.

Mathematics

In discussing work at the infant stage it was suggested that the beginnings of formal arithmetic should be postponed until children are familiar with basic ideas in number. In the junior school the basic processes require to be mastered and this means sufficient oral practice in the simpler number bonds to enable pupils to give correct answers almost automatically. However, the modern approach to mathematics in the junior school takes the standpoint that concentrating on 'doing sums' is out of place. Much of this thinking is based on the work of Piaget and others. Piaget described in his stages of intellectual growth a 'concrete operational stage' which begins about the age of seven years followed by a stage of 'propositional or formal operations' which begins at about eleven or twelve years of age. In the first stage concepts are formed only as a result of concrete experiences whereas at the second stage the adolescent is capable of beginning to formulate hypotheses and make deductions from them. He no longer needs to reason about things and events but he can reason from them. These stages of concept formation are relevant to mathematical learning.

The use of structural materials at the infant stage has already been suggested as a means of helping to develop concepts, especially notational concepts, and many of these materials can appropriately be carried on into the junior stage. The modern approach also lays stress on the provision of other experiences. These include measuring, using footrules, yardsticks and other measures; weighing through an understanding of balancing; measuring liquids with a variety of measures—spoons, cups, and jugs as well as standard measures. Fractions will arise naturally from weighing and measuring. In addition, the investigation of shapes through work with coloured paper, cardboard and shapes boards will stimulate the beginnings of geometric thinking. These suggestions are only a few of the many ideas which pervade present thinking in this subject and the reader is invited to consult specific books on this topic (23, 24).

Clearly, a great deal of the reasoning that develops through such activities as have been mentioned is facilitated by verbal thinking and the use of words. On the other hand, there is no reason to suppose that many of the appropriate concepts cannot be arrived at even when there is severe linguistic retardation. The activities also provide the opportunity to present the vocabulary associated with these mathematical concepts and the pupils should be given such terms as more than, how many more, altogether, total, difference, change, length, weight, width, depth, height, a few, some, size, distance, how long (time), and others as they arise out of their experiences. The ability to understand and use these terms and the understanding of the concepts that should have come through the work described above will enable the pupils to tackle problems. These have generally been considered to be a stumbling-block for deaf children and yet it is only through an ability to work through a problem that a child can show he really understands mathematical processes.

Good attitudes towards mathematics must be engendered in the junior school and these can only be achieved when teachers imaginatively provide first-hand experiences for the pupils, encourage them to think and express their thoughts in words about those experiences and themselves show enthusiasm for what is being done.

Other Subjects

Some of the other 'subjects' normally dealt with at the junior stage can only be mentioned here very briefly. Many teachers, in fact, believe that they should not be taught as such at this stage but integrated into centres of interest, environmental studies, social studies or some other such description. Be that as it may, and there is a strong argument in its favour for deaf children at this stage, there are some principles which are equally applicable to whatever system is used. One basic principle is that the subject should be interesting to pupils at that stage of development for which it is intended. Since deaf children are as much interested in their environment as their hearing peers, some study of their environment is an important part of the curriculum at the junior stage. The two 'subjects' which can be dealt with in this way are geography and nature study. In the lower classes of the junior school it is probably wisest not to try to distinguish clearly between them, but to utilise explorations of the environment as bases for both.

Lessons about where the food we eat comes from and how people live and what they work at in other countries will begin to widen their knowledge of the world and prepare the way for more specifically geographical studies by the time the pupils are ten or eleven years old. Many of the topics included in the headings given in this paragraph can be very usefully illustrated by means of films which should be used wherever they are appropriate.

In addition to increasing the children's knowledge of their environment, the topics noted above which are related to nature study should have as one of their aims the stimulation of careful observation. This can be done by getting the pupils to describe, as accurately as their knowledge of language permits, what they see or to reproduce what has been seen in the form of careful sketches. Stimulation of observation can come also in the later junior stages through the introduction of some elementary science teaching. Junior school children are interested in how things work and finding out about this should be one of the main aims of these science lessons. The other aims should be to help the children to observe carefully and begin to reason out why certain things happen. Topics that can be introduced at this stage include 'air' (Is it real? Where is it? Does it move? etc.); magnetism; elementary electricity; heat (effect of heat on water and other liquids and on solids, measuring heat, etc.).

In all these 'subjects' teachers of the deaf will have two main objects. One of these will be to help children to increase their knowledge of the world around them and the other will be to utilise the interest created by the subject as a motivation for talking and as a means of developing language skills. This will include the increase in vocabulary that comes from new knowledge and the practice in known sentence patterns with a wide variety of context.

History and religious education have a different purpose from the previous group of subjects and should serve to stimulate the imagination of children. They go beyond the limits of the environment and are concerned with the social and moral behaviour of mankind. It seems to be generally agreed that at the junior stage history teaching should follow two main lines. One of these is a biographical approach dealing with the lives of famous people. These may be drawn from any period in history and should not necessarily follow a chronological order. As well as introducing the pupils to some of our cultural heritage, such stories will serve to illustrate certain desirable traits such as courage, persistence, truthfulness, honesty and the like. The stories will not only be told to the children at a level of language which they can comprehend but they should give opportunities for other activities such as dramatisation, drawing and model-making. The other approach is a social one illustrating man's life through the ages and his constant struggle to improve his environment. Such topics as the development of houses, clothing, agriculture, transport and so on would be included in this approach. Here there is a need for a great variety of illustrations including film-strips which will serve to make developments plain. Neither approach is mutually exclusive and it is probably desirable during the period of the junior school to utilise both. Since a time-sense does not seem to develop until the end of the junior stage any attempt to introduce it to deaf children before the age of eleven seems likely to result in confusion. By about the end of this stage, however, the use of time-charts should be begun and the events and developments that have been dealt with placed appropriately on the time-scale.

It is quite often difficult to differentiate much of religious education from history. Stories from the Old Testament or incidents in the life of Christ are, to the pupils, just so many more historical tales. Whilst such stories are an essential background to Christian teaching, if they are to have any moral or religious value, they must be something more than that. This does not mean that the moral must be heavily underlined, but that the basis of the teaching should be to bring about a knowledge of the God-man relationship and of the teaching of Christ in relation to men's lives. A full understanding of these is, of course, quite beyond the capabilities of junior deaf children, but unless the teacher has this aim in the background and tries to lay the foundations for this understanding, it is unlikely ever to be achieved. Some possible themes on this basis might be God's call to men (Abraham, Joseph, Samuel); God's helpers (Moses, Paul, missionaries); God's Kingdom (stories told by Jesus); the teaching of Jesus (about prayer, about worship, about ourselves). Here again, illustrations, the flannelgraph, pictures drawn by pupils, and dramatisation, are activities which can be used to follow up the introductory lesson on the theme.

Although not specifically religious education, some moral teaching is also desirable. It is true that for a large part of this parents are generally expected to be responsible, but in the case of deaf children more responsibility has usually to be taken by the school than is normally the case. Reasons for this are the lack of good communication between parents and child, in some instances, and the absence from home of children at boarding schools. Here, as always, the best example is the teacher herself but children do need to have help in acquiring concepts of truthfulness, honesty, unselfishness, kindness and the other virtues as well as some training in the social graces such as politeness, good manners and cleanliness. Stories can be used as illustrations of acceptable and desirable behaviour and most of the teaching will be indirect and related to incidents in normal daily living and in games. Deaf children who have been trained to be observant and aware of the needs of others in everyday situations will thereby absorb the true meaning of courtesy. The social graces which, because of linguistic retardation, might otherwise be lacking, will consequently become more meaningful and the phrases which express them, such as 'pardon, 'will you have . . .', 'may I . . .' and 'excuse me', more readily acquired. Good social behaviour and the practice of the common courtesies of life will not only compensate for other difficulties but will help to give a deaf child poise and confidence in social situations.

The principle stated at the end of the previous section is equally applicable here. One aim of each lesson will be related to the subject matter, but another will be related to language usage and development. It is through this wide range of subject matter, all of which should be capable of arousing interest at this stage, that language can be practised and taken further, stage by stage.

SECONDARY STAGE

By the time pupils reach this stage, the range of individual differences has become even more marked than at the junior level. These intellectual differences are accentuated by the development of special abilities during the adolescent years. To cater for this wide range of intellectual abilities, special skills and also vocational aspirations, the secondary school provision in England for hearing pupils is divided into three categories whether in separate schools or separate streams in a comprehensive school. For hearing-handicapped pupils a small proportion of the most linguistically advanced and intellectually gifted are creamed off into the Mary Hare Grammar School and Burwood Park School. Apart from this group, which does not amount to more than 8 per cent of the age-groups concerned, and those who are able to participate in the three counties' scheme and take their secondary education at Nutfield Priory, pupils at the secondary stage remain at an all-age school and follow what is virtually an extension of elementary education. It is true that an increasing number of all-age schools are trying to introduce what is described as a 'secondary modern curriculum' for their older pupils but such curricula in many schools consist mainly of the primary school subjects taken to a slightly higher level plus the introduction of a little science. A Ministry of Education pamphlet (25) defines the aim of the modern school as being "to provide a good all-round secondary education, not focussed primarily on the traditional subjects of the school curriculum, but developing out of the interests of the children. Through its appeal to their interests it will stimulate their ability to learn and will teach them to pursue quality in thought, expression and craftsmanship. It will interpret the modern world to them and give them a preparation for life in the widest sense, including a full use of leisure. It will aim at getting the most out of every pupil that he is capable of, at making him adaptable, and at teaching him to do a job properly and thoroughly and not to be satisfied with bad workmanship, and to be exact in what he does and says. Freedom and flexibility are of its essence and are indeed its great opportunity." These were brave words, but in the period that has elapsed since they were written it is doubtful whether the achievements have been as high as the hopes. Indeed, pressure for some form of status, usually in the shape of a certificate on completion of the course, has led many modern schools back into the "traditional subjects of the school curriculum". This is scarcely the place to discuss whether the philosophers were right and the schools have mistaken their purpose or have been forced by external pressures into paths they would have preferred not to follow. The relevance to the present section lies in the fact that there is no clear agreement on what the function of the secondary modern school should be nor what should be the content of its curriculum. Perhaps the implementation of the proposals in the Newsom Report (33) (which, in fact, confirm the principles laid down in the 1947 pamphlet), especially those which suggest that the curriculum should be a preparation for adult life and introduce the idea of choice in the subjects studied during the last two years of schooling, will help to restore to the secondary school its true function. For deaf children it seems clear that one of its functions must be to prepare the pupils for life in an adult and changing society. There are likely to be numerous interpretations of the ways in which this can best be done, but it is suggested here that this must include the development of thinking; communication; creative work; attitudes; and social behaviour and morality. The subjects of the curriculum, however great their intrinsic worth, should be primarily thought of in terms of their contribution to the above aspects of the pupils' development. Perhaps this is just another way of expressing what was said in the Ministry of Education pamphlet and, if so, it has at least that weight of authority behind it. At any rate, it seems to the author to set out what he feels to be the greatest needs of deaf children in preparing them for life and work in society.

A brief examination of these five aspects of development may help to show how they can be related to the curriculum of the secondary stage.

Various aspects of thinking in deaf children have been the subject of considerable, although by no means exhaustive, psychological study. Apart from the rather obvious conclusion that in thought processes which involve verbal-symbolic behaviour deaf children are retarded, there is evidence that these thought processes are differently structured because of the different background of experience which a deaf child has had compared with a hearing child. In view of this Myklebust (18) has suggested that deaf children could be helped by specific training in certain types of mental operations, for example, training in memory abilities such as "memory for digits, dot patterns, bead patterns and for word sequences". Training in reasoning by analogy (father is to home as bird is to . . .), deductive reasoning and problems requiring the recognition of the relationship between cause and effect for their solution, are also suggested as mental operations for which specialised training might be given.

Observers such as Pugh (22) and Templin (26) have noted that frequently it is not the concepts themselves which trouble deaf children but the symbols in which these concepts are conveyed. Ultimately, therefore, training in thinking comes down to training deaf children to think in words. This, of course, is something that must be begun in the infant department and the directed activities which were described at that stage can be used to form part of that early training. It needs to be carried on throughout the primary stage and some of the specialised training suggested by Myklebust could appropriately be given then. At the secondary stage this training can be continued further. Obviously, subjects which are scientifically oriented are valuable as a means of providing the kind of experiences in thinking which are appropriate and interesting. Not only the subjects which are labelled as science serve this purpose, but domestic subjects, woodwork and metalwork on the one hand, and the 'arts' subjects such as history and geography on the other, can provide ample opportunities for stimulating thought and giving practice in reasoning. Whatever the subject the important thing is for the teacher to ensure that the thought can be expressed in words and for opportunities to be given for extensive practice in doing this. The UNESCO publication, *Education and Mental Health* (16) suggests that "at least up to the age of sixteen, children should be mastering more complex modes of thought and action rather than acquiring knowledge, for example of physics or chemistry or literature as such". Clearly, this thinking and doing must be related to fields of knowledge, but the stress should be on the expression of increasingly complex thought processes rather than on the memorisation of facts selected by the teacher. It is frequently noted that some teachers are too anxious to get general ideas across to their pupils and are not sufficiently concerned with

K

precision in expression. For example, "I put the salt in the water and it dissolves. The salt dissolves in the water." Here the teacher is anxious to teach the word 'dissolves' and although the statements are correct it would be more helpful to the pupils to use temporal or conditional clauses: "If I put the salt in the water it will dissolve" or "The salt dissolves when I put it in the water". Practice in using such sentences appropriately does help in learning to think precisely. Similarly, it is better to teach the pattern "Canals were built in the eighteenth century because the roads were very bad and the cost of sending goods was very high" than the statements that "In the eighteenth century roads were very bad and the cost of sending goods was high. Canals were built to carry the goods more cheaply." The last two sentences are statements of fact but the first pattern shows the causal relationship and is therefore helpful in encouraging the pupils to think clearly. Of course, these patterns require much practice before they form part of the spontaneous speech of the pupil, but this orientation of the teaching of subjects so that the pupil's mind is directed towards perceiving relationships seems to be essential if he is going to be able to use and understand language effectively. It perhaps hardly needs saying that statements of fact are very frequently appropriate: the alternative patterns suggested are emphasised because they generally seem to receive less attention despite their importance in the development of thinking.

The development of communication at this stage involves both the improvement of the pupil's own speech and his understanding of the speech of others. Beginning with the first-named, it seems better that most of the work should be done through individual lessons. Whilst all members of a staff must ensure that a pupil talks as well as he is capable of doing, it is desirable to have either a specialist teacher who can take responsibility for all speech improvement lessons or specific responsibility placed on the form master for the speech lessons of his form. At least three periods per week of twenty minutes each need to be allocated for this purpose and these could well be dovetailed with library or similar periods on the time-table. Much of what has been said about the speech improvement lessons at the junior stage is still applicable although, clearly, a more adult approach is required. Some form of phonetic script should be taught (in class lessons) so that the pupils can more readily learn to pronounce new words when the phonetic symbols are given by the teacher. At the same time, diagrams showing the positions of the speech organs in making different phonemes can be used to correct faulty positioning. Other visual aids such as pitch indicators can be used to enable the pupils to see what kind of effect they are trying to produce. It can also be helpful to let them compare the visible movements in talking which they themselves make and can see in a mirror with the movements made by an announcer on a television programme. Cutting down exaggerated movements not only greatly improves the quality and rate of the speech but makes it more socially acceptable. Since most profoundly deaf children are unable to hear their own voices by bone conduction and can only monitor them when they can hear themselves through a powerful amplifier, some practice must be given in adjusting voice level to different background conditions. These and other matters can all be dealt with at a level which is interesting to the adolescent and can therefore make the speech period something which is not an apparently dull repetition of what was done at the junior stage but has the wider appeal of the adult world to which adolescent thoughts are becoming increasingly oriented. Periodic recordings of pupils' speech still need to be made as a means of enabling the teacher to assess progress and analyse difficulties as a basis for further work. At the secondary stage it is useful practice both for spoken and written English to get pupils to prepare in writing a short talk to give to other members of the class on a specified topic. Pupils could write out and rehearse their talk as part of their 'preparation'. The speech teacher might also take the opportunity of going over the prepared material with the pupils, giving help in phrasing and in any other ways that will contribute to greater intelligibility.

The receptive side of communication will essentially include further experience in making the best use of residual hearing. In group lessons the pupils should have explanations about the working of hearing aids and the advantages and disadvantages of the different kinds. They also need to know in as precise a way as possible what they can hear and what are the limitations of their hearing. At the same time, lessons should be given to help pupils to identify the phonemes that are visible; lessons in lipreading, in fact. Pupils can be shown, without exaggeration, the shape of the mouth for different vowels, which consonants can be identified, which may be confused and, of course, which are completely invisible. Although some analysis of this kind needs to be taken as separate lessons, the combination of looking and listening needs to be stressed and practised. In the later years of the secondary stage the pupils should be encouraged to bring forward their own problems and discuss with the teacher how far and in what ways they are capable of solution. In the presentation of the talks referred to at the end of the previous paragraph, the other members of the class could at first be supplied with duplicated copies for prior reading. They would then be able to watch the speaker and listen through a group aid during the whole of the talk in the reasonable certainty that they could follow his speech with a considerable degree of accuracy. Later developments of this technique would be the prior supply of a summary only, and finally only the topic would be named before the talk began. Such lessons have the dual purpose of providing motivation for intelligible speech and practice in lipreading and aided hearing without the pupils quickly losing the sense of what was being said and becoming discouraged. It should therefore be seen that these two aspects of communication can be readily welded together in the time-table under some such title as 'Speech and Hearing'. There is adequate scope for both group and individual lessons of which there should be not less than one group and three individual lessons per week.

The next theme to be discussed is that which was given the general title of 'creative work'. This includes painting, drawing and craft work using a wide variety of materials. Such work should give the pupils the opportunity for self-expression of a non-verbal kind where their limitations are likely to be least and it should have a stabilising effect on emotional development. Adolescents have a desire to create which, if stifled, can lead to maladjustment and which should be catered for by regular periods set aside for this purpose. Because of the varieties of interests and aptitudes amongst pupils, there is a need to provide a wide variety of craft materials—wood models, clay models, models in plastics, metalwork, sewing and weaving, bookbinding and block-cutting for printing on a variety of materials, to name some of the more common types. Besides providing a significant contribution to sound mental health, these activities can often develop into interests which may affect vocational bias or develop into adult leisure-time pursuits.

For many normal hearing children the writing of prose or poetry, dramatic work, or   music provide the most satisfying means of self-expression. Whilst some of these are by no means closed to deaf children they often give rise to difficulties that adversely affect spontaneity, and on the whole it seems better to concentrate on the kind of activities listed above.

An attitude has been defined as "an enduring organisation of motives, perceptions and emotions with respect to some aspect of the individual's world" (27). Such organisations are, of course, built up early in life and form the attitudes of deaf children as seen in their behaviour in a variety of contexts. Fortunately, attitudes are not unchangeable although it is obviously better to have good attitudes from the start, thus avoiding the necessity of embarking on what may be a long-term process of effecting a change. Retardation in linguistic development tends to bring in its train social immaturity and with social immaturity comes the formation of undesirable habits and attitudes. At the same time, the attitudes of parents and society in general to deaf children react on the development of reciprocal attitudes in the latter. An over-protective attitude on the part of parents will result in over-dependence in the child and the expectation of adult help in situations where this is unnecessary and unwise. At the nursery stage a beginning should have been made in developing the right kind of attitude to other children; in the primary stage this would be developed further and an acceptable attitude to work built up. At the primary stage also, through appropriate experiences, moral attitudes in respect of such matters as honesty, truthfulness, politeness and thoughtfulness should be developed.

By the adolescent stage, therefore, most of the attitudes which a child will carry over into adult life are becoming crystallised. Moral education in respect of truth, honesty and the like must still take place, since attitudes towards such matters take on a more complex character. Does one, for example, never steal or cheat when dealing with another private individual, but take the opportunity of travelling on a bus without paying one's fare, or suppress information when filling in an income tax return, as the chance arises? Or again, may one always be honest in dealing with one's friends but sell a faulty article to a stranger? How can a socially naïve deaf adolescent be brought to face up to such problems? Practice, it is said, is better than precept, but it seems that precepts cannot be altogether out of place here. Adolescents need to be shown the kind of situations that have to be faced and how the problems can be grappled with. Practice, however, can come through teachers showing that they are completely honest and truthful in their dealings with their pupils. The co-operation of parents must be sought and their help in demonstrating the same kind of practice enlisted. It is the behaviour of parents and teachers towards these adolescents that will most effectively show them the precepts in action and help them to develop the right kind of attitudes themselves.

Attitudes towards work and responsibility are particularly important at this stage. It has often been noted that many deaf children are unwilling to work hard at seemingly uninteresting tasks. Although modern educational theory rightly seeks to enlist the interest of the pupils as an important part of the process of learning, there are facts and tables to be learned which inevitably involve somewhat dull routine work. It is not easy to explain to any child, let alone one with a severe linguistic handicap, that the ultimate goal of this uninteresting work is a satisfying one, but it is part of one's moral development to have to accept the fact that one is obliged to work assiduously even when the task is an uninteresting one. Developing a right attitude towards work and good work habits is particularly important from a vocational point of view. It may make all the difference between employment and unemployment to a deaf worker, particularly when he is a marginal worker.

Attitudes to work and the assumption of responsibility can be considered as evidence of the stage of social maturity reached. They therefore lead us into a discussion of social and emotional development—the last of the aspects on which it was suggested that stress should be laid. As with all the other aspects mentioned, they develop with the maturing personality and must be thought of before the secondary stage. The social training at the nursery stage is the basis of the school's contribution towards this development: some of the social training appropriate at the junior stage has already been described. However, much more stress must be laid on social development at the secondary level than has yet been given to it in most schools. Myklebust (18) discussing studies of the social maturity of deaf children has pointed out that most studies have shown that as deaf children grew older they became less competent socially. "After the age of fifteen social maturity entails assisting in the care of others, providing for the future and assuming responsibilities for the general welfare." It is at this level of social maturity that the deaf adolescent and young adult begin to fall well behind the normal level. Any form of handicap will result in an increased dependence on others and the attainment of social competence up to the age of about fifteen is bound up with a gradually maturing independence. It is part of the school's function to help the child to attain this independence and assume some responsibility not only for his own social behaviour but also for his learning activities. This is particularly important at the secondary stage as part of the preparation for life and work in an adult world. Pupils need to learn to work independently and without the help of the teacher. Class or group lessons, therefore, should be interspersed with periods of individual study and work. Experiments, assignments and systematic use of a well-stocked school library assume very great importance at this stage as part of the conative and affective aspects of learning. Indeed it may be said with some justification that a number of the aspects of the educational programme which have already been discussed as having special significance at the secondary stage are related to the conative and affective aspects of mental processes. Perhaps it is not untrue to suggest that in the past too much attention has been paid to the cognitive aspects of learning and that much of the ineffectiveness of some of the schooling is due to the neglect of the other two.

Emotional problems of adolescence have often been stressed, and sometimes overstressed, in relation to education at this stage. The need for social acceptance and emotional stability seem to be well-established and should be taken into consideration by the teacher. Sex education and the need to develop normal heterosexual relationships fall at least within part of the province of the school, particularly in boarding schools, although they must also be the concern of the parents. Indeed, as Lovell (28) points out, "the school and other environmental agencies are not as important as the home in these respects". Deaf adolescents who spend over 50 per cent of their school lives in boarding schools away from home are further handicapped through the limitation of home influences in these matters. It is perhaps only fair to add that many of those attending day schools are no less handicapped because of the inability of parents to communicate with them save at a very simple level. The specific problems of deaf adolescents have never yet been adequately investigated and a study of these and ways in which they and their parents can be helped to meet them is very much overdue.

At this point, the content of the curriculum within which these aspects of development require to be stressed must be mentioned. Loukes (29) rightly points out that "there is no single type of curriculum suitable for all modern schools" and Dent, writing in 1958 (30), after surveying the curricula provided in a large number of schools, found that they could be broadly classified into five main types. The largest group of schools was those which offered one or more vocationally biased courses, but the various offerings ranged from elementary school work to preparation for G.C.E. in one or more subjects.

In 1959, the National College of Teachers of the Deaf investigated the facilities available for secondary education for deaf pupils outside the two selective schools. Thirty-eight schools responded to a questionnaire and all reported the inclusion of the following subjects in their curricula: English, religious education, mathematics, physical education, geography, history, art, speech and general knowledge. Other subjects which were commonly but not universally provided were woodwork (37 schools); homecraft, 31; science, 27; needlework, 25; technical drawing, 19; metalwork, 15; typewriting, 10; commercial subjects, 7. Exceptionally, the following courses were provided: rural science, motor maintenance and boot repairing. The actual level to which these subjects were taught and the content of the syllabi were not reported and it is to be expected that there were very wide variations in both. This is substantiated by the report that only one-third of the schools offering science had a special room for this purpose and only one-fifth of the rooms used for technical drawing were specially equipped for it. Restrictions on the provision of courses were also brought about by an inadequate supply of specialist teachers. In the thirty-eight responding schools there was a total of forty teachers who were qualified as teachers of the deaf and also in specialist subjects. There were another seventy-four specialist teachers with subject qualifications but no qualifications as teachers of the deaf. It seems, therefore, that schools for the deaf have certainly made a beginning in providing a variety of courses at the secondary stage but, compared with secondary schools for hearing pupils, there is a serious shortage of qualified specialist teachers and appropriately equipped classrooms and laboratories. It also seems to be true that in very few cases have the subjects been welded into a coherent course. It would be very desirable to co-ordinate a number of courses so that the interrelationship was apparent and so that the group had a vocational or other thematic orientation.

Wollman (31) making proposals along these lines has suggested a homecraft course and a technical course and has given details of suggested syllabi for them. To these might be added others such as arts and crafts or commercial courses. Schools, depending on their size and the availability of specialist teachers, might offer one, two or three options, but it could not be expected that any one school could offer a complete range. Planning on a regional basis would prevent overlaps and ensure the provision was as complete as possible within a region, so that pupils wishing a course not supplied in the school which they had hitherto attended could be transferred at the secondary stage to a school offering the course of their choice. Although arrangements such as these might prove unpopular with some parents since they would necessitate some pupils who had hitherto attended day schools moving to boarding schools, they seem to be the only rational solution to the problem of giving deaf children opportunities for a secondary education that is comparable with what is provided for hearing children and suitable as a preparation for adult life. Indeed, it seems likely that nothing less than the provision of coherent courses at the secondary stage can effectively meet the educational and psychological needs of adolescent deaf pupils.

Connor and Rosenstein (32) in a study of the jobs undertaken by deaf female school leavers conclude by suggesting that vocational education for girls must "assume a more serious and vital role in the school programme". But the vocational education they suggest would include many academic subjects including reading, writing, social studies, science and mathematics, and the writers argue that a properly planned curriculum on these lines would lead to emotional stability and social maturity as well as to adequate vocational orientation. They also call for more adequate vocational guidance and this is a demand which the present writer would most strongly support. It seems true to say that there is virtually no systematic and planned vocational guidance taking place in schools at present, and that a very strong case can be made out for the appointment of a member of staff for this purpose either on a full-time or a part-time basis in every school where there is a secondary department. Such an appointment might well serve, in addition, to highlight some of the weaknesses in an existing curriculum and point to ways in which it could be strengthened so that pupils might be more adequately prepared for work.

It is perhaps worth noting that, after the above paragraphs had been written, it was found that the Newsom Report (33) raises similar points about the content of the curriculum. It points out that one of the most urgent questions which schools have to ask themselves is about "the total patterns of the curriculum, for all their pupils. They are finding that it is not enough to tinker with the separate pieces." Indeed, a great deal of that report has very great relevance to the present section and many of the recommendations, if implemented, would revolutionise secondary education for deaf pupils.

Wollman, in the study already referred to, went on to propose the introduction of some form of leaving certificate for deaf pupils. He believed that this would lead to an improvement in standards and act as an incentive to the pupils. In order to plan for such a certificate he analysed the attainments of deaf pupils between the age of fourteen and sixteen years in fourteen schools for the deaf and partially hearing. In both English and arithmetic the pupils showed considerable retardation compared with hearing pupils of the same age, but perhaps of more significance were the wide differences between the mean scores of pupils from different schools. Wollman suggests that these could be due to poor and unstimulating out-of-school conditions, the lack of provision for secondary education and the low standards of aspiration set for the pupils by the school. These are challenging statements and there seems little doubt that such deficiencies do exist and that, until they are met, little improvement in levels of attainment will be made. The provision of integrated courses which are interesting to the pupils and within which stress is laid on the aspects of development already referred to is suggested here as being the most helpful way of tackling the problems of secondary education for deaf children. The establishment of some form of separate leaving certificate is more debatable. The use of external pressures to provide motivation is not altogether satisfactory and, although the award of a certificate would signify a certain level of attainment, it seems more important to encourage the development of more mature ways of thinking, behaving and feeling than to make levels of knowledge the goals for the pupils. An increase in maturity will eventually bring about higher levels of attainment either at school or after and will be reflected in a much more satisfactory adjustment to adult life within the community than an extension of factual knowledge can by itself bring.

Proposals for the new Certificate of Secondary Education are somewhat more promising. Here, it is planned that external pressures will be minimised and the pupils will receive certificates if they show that they have satisfactorily completed the courses they have taken. So long as the 'examination' is an assessment of the work that the pupils have done on their courses, it would certainly meet the objections that were raised to the introduction of a leaving certificate for schools for the deaf. The courses would, of course, have to be approved by the examining boards but this would in many ways be an advantage rather than a disadvantage. Already, some heads of schools are showing interest in the possibilities of this development and it is likely that liaisons will be made with regional examining boards to investigate ways in which secondary departments in schools for the deaf may be associated with the scheme.

REFERENCES

1 Murphy, K. P. (1957). 'Tests of Abilities and Attainments'. Chap. 11 in *Educational Guidance and the Deaf Child* (ed. Ewing). Manchester Univ. Press

2 Dale, D. M. C. (1962). *Applied Audiology for Children*. Thomas, Springfield, Illinois

3 Goodman, A. I. (1949). 'Capacity to Hear of Pupils in Schools for the Deaf'. *J. of Laryng. and Otol.* 63, 551

4 Ewing, E. C. (1963). 'Some Psychological Variables in the Training of Young Deaf Children'. *Volta Review*, 65, 68

5 Pickles, A. M. (1957). 'Home Training with Hearing Aids'. Chap. 4 (ii) *Educational Guidance and the Deaf Child*

6 National Association for Mental Health (1955). *Periods of Stress in the Primary School*

7 Groht, M. A. (1958). *Natural Language for Deaf Children*. Alex. Graham Bell Assoc. for the Deaf, Washington

8 De Lissa, L. (1939). *Life in the Nursery School*. Longmans, Green & Co.

9 Gesell, A. & Ilg, F. L. (1946). *The Child from Five to Ten*. Hamish Hamilton

10 Ministry of Education (1950). *Reading Ability*. Pamphlet No. 18. HMSO

11 Schonell, F. J. (1946). *The Psychology and Teaching of Reading.* Oliver & Boyd

12 Ewing, I. R. & A. W. G. (1954). *Speech and the Deaf Child.* Manchester Univ. Press

13 Huizing, H. C. (1964). 'The Significance of Cybernetic Phenomena in Audiology'. *Progress on Biocybernetics,* Vol. I (ed. Wiener & Schadé). Elsevier Publ. Co., Amsterdam

14 Newsom, J. H. (1950). *The Child at School.* Penguin Books

15 *Report of the Consultative Committee on the Primary School* (1931). HMSO

16 Wall, W. D. (1955). *Education and Mental Health.* UNESCO. Harrap

17 Brereton, B. Le G. (1957). *The Schooling of Children with Impaired Hearing.* Commonwealth Office of Education, Sydney, Australia

18 Myklebust, H. R. (1960). *The Psychology of Deafness.* Grune & Stratton, New York

19 Hart, B. O. (1963). *Teaching Reading to Deaf Children.* Alex. Graham Bell Assoc. for the Deaf, Washington

20 Russell, D. H. & Karp, E. E. (1960). *Reading Aids Through the Grades.* Teachers' College, Columbia University

21 Scottish Education Department (1950). *The Primary School in Scotland.* HMSO, Edinburgh

22 Pugh, B. (1960). 'Developing the Deaf Child's Power of Reasoning'. *Volta Review,* 62, 334

23 Sealey, L. G. W. (1962). *The Creative Use of Mathematics in the Junior School.* Blackwell

24 Churchill, E. M. (1961). *Counting and Measuring.* Routledge & Kegan Paul

25 Ministry of Education (1947). *The New Secondary Education.* Pamphlet No. 9. HMSO

26 Templin, M. (1961). Personal communication on current research in the Univ. of Minnesota

27 Peel, E. A. (1956). *The Psychological Bases of Education.* Oliver & Boyd

28 Lovell, K. (1961). *Educational Psychology and Children.* Univ. of London Press Ltd.

29 Loukes, H. (1956). *Secondary Modern.* Harrap

30 Dent, H. C. (1958). *Secondary Modern Schools.* Routledge & Kegan Paul

31 Wollman, D. C. (1961). *Some Problems involved in the Applica-*

tion of *Secondary Modern Education for Deaf Pupils*. Unpublished thesis, Univ. of Manchester Library

32 Connor, L. & Rosenstein, J. (1963). 'Vocational Status and Adjustment of Deaf Women'. *Volta Review*, 65, 585

33 Report of General Advisory Council for Education (1963). *Half Our Future*. HMSO

6

The education of partially hearing children

At the beginning of the previous chapter an attempt was made to define what was meant by a child who was deaf in the educational sense of the word. Partially hearing pupils can therefore be described simply as those who have a hearing handicap amounting to less than 'deafness'. We have already seen that, in terms of the statutory definition, they have enough hearing to acquire some speech and language naturally, and they may include children who have become deaf adventitiously after normal spoken language has been acquired. It will thus be apparent that the term 'partially hearing' covers children with a very wide range of hearing losses in addition to the other variables that will have a bearing upon the most appropriate educational treatment. In Chapter 3 there were set out suggested criteria for placement which would take into account these matters in allocating children to schools. It is usually assumed that the children who are less handicapped by their impairment will stay in an ordinary school whilst those with greater handicaps will need special educational treatment. Although this assumption is generally true, there seems to be a very considerable overlap between the two categories not only in terms of hearing loss but also in terms of abilities and attainments.

In this chapter we will look at representative children in these two types of educational environment and consider the kind of help they require to meet their differing needs.

PARTIALLY HEARING CHILDREN IN ORDINARY SCHOOLS

Although these children were classified into a separate group in the Report of the Consultative Committee into Problems

Relating to Children with Defective Hearing (1938) and suggestions were there made about the kind of help they were likely to need, little, in fact, was done to provide that help until after World War II. In that Report they were referred to as Grade IIA and it was recommended that they should have a favourable position in class, an individual hearing aid, or tuition in lipreading, or any combination of these. This help was to be given either by attendance for one or two periods per week at a special class or by visits from a peripatetic teacher.

So far as can be ascertained no local authority in Britain appointed peripatetic teachers until 1948. Since that time the rate of growth of this service was very slow until about 1958 when many more local authorities began to appoint them. At present there are about one hundred specially qualified teachers employed in this way. Assisting partially hearing pupils attending ordinary schools seems to be only one of three main functions which such teachers have. They are also usually given responsibility for attending clinics at which diagnosis of deafness is made and recommendations for placement discussed. Their third function is generally to give guidance to parents of pre-school deaf children. As a consequence of this tripartite role the time left for remedial help to partially hearing pupils is small and is often spent in advising classroom teachers of the difficulties which individual partially hearing pupils experience and suggesting ways in which the pupils can be helped. This, of course, is a valuable and necessary service although it does not make for a very great deal of direct contact with the pupil nor give him enough of the expert help which he may require.

It seems to be generally true to say that this interest in the problems of partially hearing pupils in ordinary schools is a post-1945 development. This is true not only of Britain but of other countries also, and, indeed, not very many other countries are yet in a position to provide for the needs of children whose handicaps are relatively less severe. In Denmark, since 1950, when hard of hearing pupils could be supplied with a hearing aid by one of the three state hearing centres, provision has been made to train teachers in ordinary schools at special summer classes to give appropriate help through auditory training and lipreading. These teachers are notified when children living in their area are diagnosed as partially hearing at the centre and are required to visit the children and made arrangements to help them. Progress reports are periodically submitted to the centre as a means of checking on suitability of placement or other requirements. The work, therefore, is undertaken not by specially qualified teachers of the deaf, as in Britain, but by trained teachers who have had a little supplementary training to enable them to do it as a small addition to their ordinary work.

In the United States of America there is no general system of dealing with this problem. The State of Iowa, for example, in 1961 began a two-year pilot investigation by appointing a peripatetic teacher of the deaf to help about twenty-two hard of hearing children attending schools in a rural area. Provisional results have shown a considerable improvement in the 'grades' of the pupils as well as much parental satisfaction with the experiment. In the City of New York lipreading and auditory training are given to hard of hearing pupils by teachers who are based on Junior High School 47, the special school provided by the City authorities to deal with all hearing-handicapped children in their area. The State of Michigan in 1950 began a short-term aural rehabilitation programme for its partially hearing pupils. They were enrolled as a special group for a six-week session in the Michigan School for the Deaf. The programme consisted of improvement in communication skills through lipreading, auditory training and speech improvement, as well as ordinary class subjects. The pupils brought their own school books with them so that they did not fall behind whilst absent from their home school. A careful follow-up was made and refresher courses organised where necessary. The programme still continues with approximately thirty-eight pupils being given help each year.

These are examples of ways in which provision is being made to meet the needs of these children. Each probably meets the particular needs of its own society but it is important to recognise that there is no single cut-and-dried method of making this provision and there is need to experiment in different ways in order to find out which gives the greatest help to the children in a particular area. The Council for Exceptional Children, in the United States, has issued a special monograph in their series The Administration of Special Education in Small School Systems dealing with hearing-handicapped children. This is, of course, written for American administrative systems but there is much that is relevant to the establishment of a comprehensive programme for such children in an English local authority area, dealing as it does with identification, the educational programme and general administration.

It is perhaps important at this point to look at the reasons why it is considered necessary to give some help to these pupils. They have been classified as being able to make satisfactory progress in an ordinary school and, whilst it is true that a minority are able to do this without any outside assistance, many of these pupils do require some part-time help or some special consideration in order to be able to remain there.

Some children are described as 'born lipreaders'. There may be an element of truth in this description but skilled help is generally required to make them even better, whilst for those who are not so fortunately endowed a good deal of training is necessary. Making the most of a hearing aid is also something that requires much training. Children have to learn to interpret imperfect patterns, to fill in sounds they cannot hear, to link sounds with their sources and to ignore unwanted noise. All this requires special training and it is essential for effective use of hearing aids. A number of partially hearing children attending ordinary schools also have defective speech. It may be intelligible but there are articulatory defects which require treatment.

These are all problems of communication, but the cumulative effects of communication disorders can be seen in educational retardation. It is true that a pupil whose retardation is greater than about two years requires more than the part-time help suggested above, but there are others whose retardation may be small but who require remedial help to close the gap or at least prevent it from becoming greater. For these reasons, therefore, it is unwise to assume that a hard of hearing pupil can be placed in an ordinary school without steps being taken to provide whatever help he may need. In Chapter 3 a classification of types of services was given which indicated that a single system was not adequate to meet the varied needs of pupils who might be able to attend ordinary schools despite their hearing impairment. It was suggested there that at least two different types of service were required and that there might well be variation in the amount of help given within these two types.

Johnson (1) has made the most comprehensive study to date of the problems of partially hearing pupils in ordinary schools in England. He suggested that there might be two per thousand school children with a marked bilateral perceptive impairment

L

not requiring special schooling and a further ten per thousand with a marked conductive hearing loss requiring either medical treatment or educational supervision or both. In a detailed study of a group of pupils with a perceptive impairment attending ordinary schools in Cheshire he found the mean hearing loss for the middle range of frequencies to be 54 db; that the majority of the pupils had a high frequency loss; and that familial deafness and meningitis accounted for more than a third of the cases, 41 per cent of the total having an unknown etiology. Their educational attainments showed varying degrees of retardation: in reading only 34 per cent were of average or above average ability, 26 per cent were between one and two years retarded and 40 per cent were retarded by over two years; in arithmetic 43·5 per cent were of average or above average ability, 31 per cent were between one and two years retarded and 25·5 per cent were retarded by over two years. Only 18 per cent of the the group had normal articulation of speech and 12 per cent had a serious impairment. 53 per cent of the group were socially adjusted, 8 per cent were maladjusted and the remainder showed symptoms of unsettledness.

This, it seems, is a gloomy picture and unfortunately the evidence is borne out from other sources. Brereton (2), in a study of 90 rubella children in Australia, reported that even these pupils whose hearing loss was around 45 db showed considerable retardation in attainments—a retardation amounting to three and a half years in knowledge of words, six years in the use of words, six and a half years in understanding spoken language, two years in mechanical reading ability and four years in understanding what was read. She concluded that "although some aspects of experience in a normal class make for success, some of the activities of such classes are likely to be so difficult for children with impaired hearing that they are unlikely to play any real part in them". Goetzinger (3) has reported on the attainments of a group of pupils in Kansas with a perceptive loss of 30–35 db. He found low levels of speech discrimination, generally some speech defects and linguistic retardation of at least one year and sometimes more. He argued the need for early identification, diagnosis and training. Kodman (4) reporting on the attainments of one hundred hard of hearing children in the public schools of Kentucky stated that they were retarded educationally by one to two and a half years. He believed that the gap between educational attainment and potential was a result of "the failure to grapple realistically with the educational needs of the hard of hearing school-age child".

All this evidence seems to confirm that the child with a relatively 'mild' hearing impairment can frequently have problems when educated in an ordinary school environment. The basic problem stems from the fact that these children are unable to hear clearly in the classroom and to follow with certainty what is said by the teacher. Brereton, in the work previously quoted (p. 198), puts her finger on the point when she says that "If one considers the qualities of the sounds occurring in a normal class, it does not seem a particularly good place for hearing words, nor a place likely to provide frequent experience of listening to language that can readily be understood". Sanders (5) when investigating the actual level of noise in classrooms found that the mean level for infant rooms was 69 db, for junior rooms 59 db and for rooms in secondary schools 62 db. The present writer found in a classroom of forty pupils aged seven to eight years the average noise level during a period of individual written work to be 55 db with peaks about 10 db above that. Since the level of the teacher's voice seldom exceeded 65 db it will be apparent that this 10 db (or less) signal to noise ratio gave little opportunity to a hearing aid user to discriminate speech with any degree of accuracy. A recording of a speech test was made under these conditions and when it was played to a group of normal hearing adults listening monaurally their discrimination scores averaged 53 per cent compared with 98 per cent in a similar test list recorded in good acoustic conditions. A group of partially hearing pupils scored 35 per cent and 85 per cent respectively in the same tests. The poor acoustic conditions of the ordinary classroom, therefore, must be considered to be a highly significant factor in the lower levels of attainments of these pupils. It is directly related to their understanding of words and through this to the understanding of ideas, use of words and increase in knowledge in general.

Some cases may illustrate difficulties and variations in discrimination in some of these children. They will also indicate the wide range of hearing impairment which is found in children attending ordinary schools.

Case 1 is a girl of 11 who has normal hearing in the better ear up to 1,000 c.p.s.; thereafter it falls off quite quickly. She has a

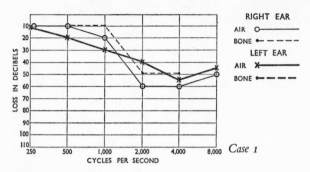

Case 1

twin sister with normal hearing. Her tonsils and adenoids have been removed but there is a residual sensory-neural loss. Her speech discrimination at 70 db is 76 per cent. She was late in

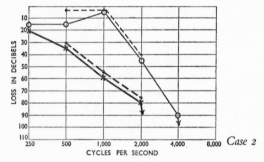

Case 2

beginning to talk, is retarded somewhat in attainments and misses quite a lot of what her teacher says in class.

Case 2 is a girl of 7 who also has good hearing in the better ear to 1,000 c.p.s. It falls off, too, rapidly thereafter. Hearing in

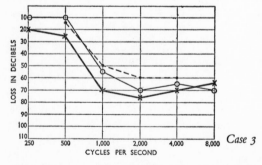

Case 3

the other ear is less good than in case 1 but with simple material she can discriminate with 100 per cent accuracy at conversational

level. Her school report says she is making good progress but her
own speech is defective for the high-frequency consonants.

Case 3 is a girl of 10 who has normal hearing up to 500 c.p.s.
and thereafter it falls off very rapidly. She discriminates with
only 64 per cent accuracy at 70 db. However, she is an intelligent
girl (I.Q. 118) and her attainments are above average—Reading
Quotient 110, Arithmetic Quotient 104. She hopes to be selected
at 11+ for a grammar school education.

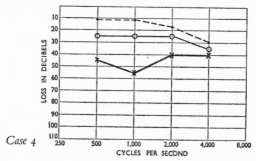

Case 4

Case 4 is a boy of 8 whose hearing loss in the better ear is
between 25 and 35 db. His deafness is of mixed type and he finds
considerable difficulty in discriminating speech. His score at a
conversational voice level is only 68 per cent and with a hearing
aid on the poorer ear this only rises to 72 per cent. He is rather a
dull boy (W.I.S.C. I.Q.=86) but his attainments are comparable
with his mental age (Reading Quotient 87; Arithmetic Quotient
92). His speech is slightly defective and he is embarrassed when
he wears a hearing aid.

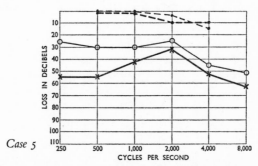

Case 5

Case 5 is a girl of 5 years with a conductive deafness of 25–45
db in the better ear. Her speech discrimination at 65 db is only
68 per cent. She is not significantly linguistically retarded but

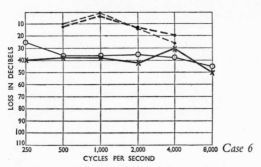

Case 6

her own speech, though intelligible, has a number of consonant omissions and substitutions.

Case 6 is a girl of 10 who has a bilateral conductive deafness, both ears having a similar loss of 30–40 db. She is a bright girl (Reading Quotient 117; Arithmetic Quotient 108) but at 70 db she can only discriminate speech with 56 per cent accuracy.

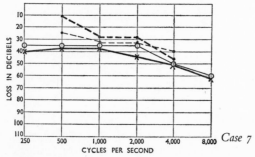

Case 7

Case 7 is a girl of 7 who has a sensory-neural loss of 35–40 db in the better ear. Over the past twelve months her hearing has

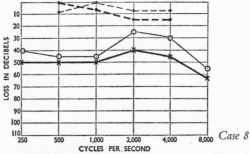

Case 8

been showing signs of deteriorating. In good acoustic conditions she scores 90 per cent in a speech discrimination test at a level of

65 db.; in a reverberant room her score drops to 55 per cent at the same level, illustrating quite dramatically how difficult she finds distinguishing what her teacher is saying in the classroom.

Case 8 is a girl of 11 years with a bilateral conductive loss of 25–45 db. Her tonsils and adenoids have been removed but this has brought about no improvement in her hearing. Her speech discrimination score at 65 db is 40 per cent and her own speech is deteriorating and her school work shows no progress.

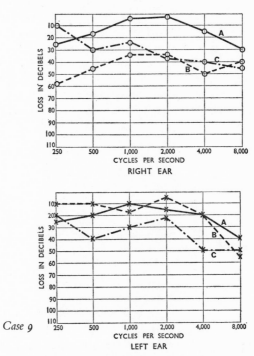

Case 9

Case 9 is a boy of 6 with a bilateral conductive loss. It fluctuates a good deal and despite medical treatment is tending to worsen rather than improve. The three audiograms illustrated were taken over a period of nine months and show these changes. (They are lettered A, B and C in chronological order). His speech discrimination scores correspondingly fluctuated from 100 per cent at 50 db in October 1962 to 30 per cent at the same level in July 1963.

The last three cases are illustrative of monaural losses in school children:

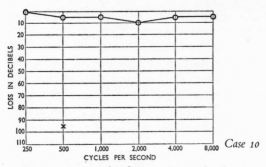

Case 10

Case 10 is a girl of 14 years with almost total deafness in the left ear, although normal hearing in the right. Onset of deafness seems to have been when she was eleven years old, possibly as the result of measles. She discriminates readily quiet speech in good acoustic conditions but experiences considerable difficulty in noise. She is two and a half years retarded in reading and arithmetic and is in a D stream in school.

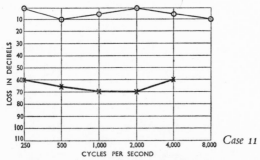

Case 11

Case 11 is a boy of 12 with normal hearing in the right ear and a severe loss in the left ear, probably resulting from measles or mumps. He, too, manages without difficulty in quiet conditions but has

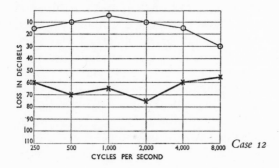

Case 12

trouble in noise. His I.Q. is 104 and he is much less retarded than Case 10 but he is quite obviously under a great deal of strain at school.

Case 12 is an intelligent boy of 8 with a slight conductive loss in the right ear and a severe sensory-neural loss in the left following measles at the age of 5. In a reverberant room he can discriminate speech with 88 per cent accuracy and is managing well in an ordinary primary school.

These examples from cases seen in our clinic could be multiplied many times. They show how unwise it is to generalise about the problems of hearing-handicapped children attending ordinary schools. Of course, from what has been said in the notes it is evident that some of these children are in any case not appropriately placed where they are. This, however, is not always the result of wrong recommendations having been made. Inappropriate placement may in some cases be due to parental refusal to accept a change and the unwillingness of a local authority to press the case; in others it may be due to the fact that there is no special help available locally and the alternative to attendance at an ordinary school is full-time special schooling in a boarding school. In this latter instance the disadvantages of retardation and placement in the C (or D) stream of an ordinary school have to be set against the disadvantages of attendance at a special school as a boarder. Such a choice illustrates the inadequacy of much of the provision for partially hearing children and the dilemma that can face those responsible for placement.

It does not follow that the majority of these children should not be allowed to remain in ordinary schools if the head teacher is prepared to accept them, but it does clearly indicate that most of them require some kind of help and support. In the first place, the ability of the child should be known to the school staff. If he wears an aid not only should members of the staff see that it is properly maintained and worn regularly, but they should be aware of its limitations and the conditions under which its use is most advantageous. If the child, as most of them do, requires to supplement hearing by watching the speaker the school staff should see that he is favourably placed to do so. Penalties should not be imposed for not hearing and, as far as possible, steps should be taken to check that the child is understanding what is required and not falling behind in his work through lack of comprehension. If speech is defective then arrangements must be made for speech therapy.

In view of these requirements it seems essential that the heads and staffs of schools where partially hearing pupils are enrolled should receive advice. It is in this capacity as adviser that a peripatetic teacher can serve a most useful function in respect of those pupils who do not need help as much as special consideration. It is not necessary for the peripatetic teacher to work with the child and, after the initial advice is given, a termly visit to ensure that all is going well is probably all that is required.

There is a further group of children with partial hearing losses for whom no provision at all appears to be made. Indeed, there has been no acknowledgement so far that their loss constitutes an educational problem. This is the group of children between the ages of five and eight who suffer from temporary conductive losses. The number of children in this group might possibly vary from region to region dependent upon the extent of catarrhal conditions, but in at least two districts in which surveys have been made (a county in North Wales and an industrial town in north-west England) of five-year-old children, the incidence has been found to be as high as 10 per cent at the time of testing. In most cases the loss is temporary in that it is present for several periods of a few weeks each between October and April and in a majority of cases the children 'grow out of it' by the time they are about eight years old. Sometimes the loss is immediately responsive to medical or surgical treatment, but more frequently it continues sporadically over a period of years. The extent of the loss is usually about 30 to 40 db in the speech range of frequencies and in at least half of the cases it seems to be bilateral. During the periods when this loss is present the children are being handicapped in their schooling at the critical time when the foundations of skills are being laid.

In view of the number of children that are involved (at least in some areas) it is not easy to suggest the best way of dealing with the educational problems. First of all, it is clear that routine hearing checks, by sweep frequency tests, should be made by trained and experienced testers and that the children found to have losses must be examined by an otologist and remain under his care until the deafness disappears and they can be discharged. Those children whose hearing defects do not respond immediately to medical or surgical treatment must be made known to their class teachers. They should then be given extra help to ensure that they have understood what has been taught and that they are not falling behind because they have not heard adequately. This, of course, presupposes smaller infant classes so that teachers can give time to the individual needs of pupils. With the present shortage of teachers it seems unlikely that the size of infant classes will be reduced and yet without this it is difficult to see how these children can get the extra help they require. An additional member of staff to deal with the problems of these and other slightly or temporarily handicapped children would be very desirable and it may be that this is a matter which should receive high priority despite staffing problems. At this stage, however, perhaps the most important matter is to have the existence and size of this problem recognised so that infant teachers and educational administrators can consider in what ways this help can best be provided.

For children who are rather more handicapped than the groups discussed above, but are not so handicapped or retarded that they require full-time special help, the services of a peripatetic teacher must be provided on a regular basis. These children may need help in learning to discriminate speech; they may need help in improving their own speech; and they may need special teaching to improve their skill in reading, in arithmetic, or in extending their vocabularies. It is arguable how much of this remedial work should be undertaken by the peripatetic teacher and how much should be left to the school itself or other remedial service. It is of less importance from what source this remedial help comes than the fact that it is provided. It may be better, in view of the many demands on the time of peripatetic teachers of the deaf, to confine their help to the improvement of communication skills, but if no other remedial help is given the child is not likely to make a great deal of progress. Authorities who do not provide remedial services must ensure that the case load of the peripatetic teacher is low enough to enable him to give each pupil who needs it an adequate amount of help.

A further very important function of the peripatetic teacher is to give advice and help to parents of pupils who come under his care. The parents need to be aware of the problems imposed by their child's hearing loss and to be given advice on ways of helping him at home. They need to be given information about hearing aids, their maintenance, volume settings, where they are most and least effective and other facts which will enable them to help their child to make the most of his aid. Ways in which they can help their children's spoken language and develop their vocabularies should be suggested, as well as help in coping with some of the behaviour problems that may arise.

While much of the advice that needs to be given to parents is best done on an personal basis specific to the parents' individual problems, there is much to be said, where parents do not live too far apart to come together occasionally, for having, say, monthly meetings where topics of general interest can be introduced and where parents can have an opportunity of sharing their problems. This makes economical use of the teacher's time and it can provide for the valuable interaction of people with similar problems.

There also seems much to be argued in favour of a short rehabilitation course for pupils similar to that described earlier in this chapter. It would be a very valuable experiment if a local authority in this country would examine its possibilities as a means of rapid concentrated help to get children who have been diagnosed as having a partial loss of hearing started on the right lines. Such a course would naturally require the follow-up services of a peripatetic teacher but it might in the end be a very economical as well as a very effective means of helping the children.

From what has been said about the manifold functions of peripatetic teachers it seems clear that they require some kind of specialist training. Whilst basic training and qualifications as a teacher of the deaf and partially hearing is an essential requirement, such training by itself does not provide for all the tasks outlined above. Additionally, there seem to be required considerable audiological knowledge, a knowledge of the attainments of unhandicapped pupils, ability to undertake remedial work and some skill in applying the principles of adult education to communicate with parents and school staffs effectively. This would appear to call for an additional comprehensive course of training to which only experienced qualified teachers of the deaf who fulfil these requirements would be admitted.

PARTIALLY HEARING CHILDREN IN SPECIAL SCHOOLS AND CLASSES

In Chapter 1 it was pointed out that the provision of separate schools and classes for partially hearing pupils has been a post-war development. On the one hand, four boarding schools for partially hearing pupils have been established at strategic points in England, and, on the other, an increasing number of local authorities have established classes of partially hearing pupils, often described as 'units', attached to ordinary county primary and county secondary schools. It has never been clear whether these two types of provision were intended to deal with children with the same degree of handicap or whether they were provided for less and more severely handicapped partially hearing pupils. The views of the writer on this matter have been expressed in Chapter 3, but authorities have never, in general, been so explicit as to the category of pupils for whom the services were intended. Some authorities make no day school provision in classes for their partially hearing pupils, so that those of the latter who cannot manage in an ordinary school even with the help of a peripatetic teacher must go to a boarding school. Other authorities provide peripatetic teachers and 'units' for partially hearing pupils and expect all of the latter to be educated in either of these two ways. It would seem that these authorities assume that the units and the boarding schools cater for the same type of pupil and by the provision of the former there is no need for them to send children to the latter. Other authorities, whilst not providing a boarding school themselves, send some of their pupils to units and others to a boarding school. These authorities thereby recognise that there is a difference in the kind of provision and that some partially hearing children are more appropriately educated in a unit and others in a boarding special school.

In view of this divergence of opinion it seems desirable to investigate the kind of children admitted to these two types of educational milieu and see if, and in what ways, they appear to be different. One obvious point of comparison is in terms of hearing loss and the information given below in Table 9 may serve to throw some light on this matter. Group A is a class of pupils in a boarding special school for partially hearing children. They were aged six to seven years when the audiograms were made. Groups B and C are classes of partially hearing children in two separate units provided by two different local education authorities: the children are also approximately seven years old. In all cases the threshold of hearing is given for the better ear only.

As a simple means of comparison the average threshold for the frequencies 250–4,000 c.p.s. may be taken for Group A and compared with the average thresholds at the same frequencies for Groups B and C combined. On this basis it will be seen that

Table 9   Comparison of pure-tone losses of pupils in a special boarding school and pupils in two units for the partially hearing

Group		Frequency					
		250	500	1,000	2,000	4,000	8,000
A	A	30	40	50	60	60	50
	B	35	55	55	95	90	N.R.
	C	40	75	80	65	50	60
	D	55	60	95	80	95	N.R.
	E	50	70	95	80	95	80
	F	0	40	70	100	N.R.	N.R.
	G	75	75	100	85	95	N.R.
	H	20	45	95	80	N.R.	N.R.
	J	40	60	70	65	70	65
	K	5	10	65	65	50	30
Average		34·0	53·0	77·5	79·5	80·5	
B	A	20	25	40	90	70	—
	B	30	55	45	55	80	—
	C	30	50	55	55	60	—
	D	50	60	65	70	70	—
	E	85	70	85	75	65	—
C	A	40	50	55	55	85	75
	B	40	60	65	65	50	45
	C	30	35	65	65	55	70
	D	20	35	55	105	95	95
Average		36·3	48·9	58·9	70·6	70·0	

the pupils in the boarding school have, on average, a markedly greater hearing loss, except at the two lower frequencies, than the pupils in the units. However, as was pointed out in Chapter 3, placement does not depend entirely upon the degree of hearing loss. Without careful, standardised measures, comparative assessments of linguistic development, speech, attainments and ability to follow speech by lipreading and/or hearing are not possible. Such information was not available but some general impressions about these factors may give a broad indication of the comparative handicaps. On the whole, the boarding school pupils had a less natural quality in their voices than the pupils in the units. The latter had many articulation problems, e.g. difficulties with 's' and 'z' (tʃɛɪns for 'changes' and sᵗɒft for 'soft') but their voices tended to be natural and intonation patterns normal. The boarding school pupils have these articulatory problems too, but their voice quality was often nearer that of deaf children. The linguistic development at the age of six years of the unit pupils tended to be further advanced than that of the special school pupils although assessment here is difficult without the use of standardised tests and the overlap between the two groups appeared to be rather greater. The special school pupils tended to be better at comprehending the speech of others through lipreading whilst the unit pupils could follow more through their hearing. In general, the unit pupils seemed to have the edge on the special school pupils in terms of comprehension. This rather superficial and subjective judgment does not, of course, give a complete picture of the situation. In any case, the variations in types of pupils attending units are very great so that what has been noted in two units will not necessarily hold for all children similarly placed. Further substance is added to this opinion from the investigation undertaken by Mutch (6) in which he found that the oral and written English of a group of older partially hearing pupils in a unit was no less good, in many respects, than that of the hearing pupils in the secondary school to which the unit was attached. It is true that the hearing pupils came from a much poorer socio-economic environment than the partially hearing pupils so that his results also show the effect of environment on the use of English.

The general impression created from the above findings and opinions is that the two types of provision do cater for different categories of pupils. This being so, attempts by authorities to place all their partially hearing pupils in one or the other type of provision are unsatisfactory from every point of view. Let us examine some of the needs of the pupils in each of the two types of provision, the aspirations which are reasonable for them and the curriculum that could be expected to meet these needs and aspirations.

Special Classes or Units

In an amusing account of her childhood Frances Warfield (7) describes some of her difficulties and the ways in which she tried to overcome them:

I heard better when I could see people's faces: therefore I heard better in the light than in the dark. In firelit rooms or summer evenings on the porch I would fall into a reverie or pretend to go to sleep. . . .

I knew dozens of ways to get people to repeat what they had said without actually asking. . . .

I was a day-dreamer and a wool-gatherer; I faked absent-mindedness, boredom, indifference. I faked illness. Fake fainting spells got me out of many a jam.

In these extracts and in many other passages she describes the elaborate defence mechanism she had built up to prevent people from knowing that she had defective hearing. It is clear, of course, that the only person she fooled was herself. Underlying the humour, however, there is the pathos of a partially hearing child facing all sorts of communication problems without being willing to admit even to herself that there were problems. In many ways such a picture reflects the problems of the pupils attending the special units attached to hearing schools. 'Hearing and not hearing', they get very imperfect patterns of what has been said and this is reflected in their own speech and use of English. Thus, a girl in such a unit when shown a plastic measure for liquids said "oo pla:tik", and when asked what it was for replied "for to measure how long". Another pupil when asked to describe the action of a classmate who was pouring some water into a dish replied "pour in de dish". In addition to the poor patterns received and uttered, the child tends to be under considerable emotional stress because of the uncertainty created by these difficulties. Because a child may hear the sound of voice quite well (e.g. B.A. and C.D. in Table 9) it is assumed by adults lacking in understanding of his difficulties that he can hear everything and therefore he may be dubbed as lazy, stupid or inattentive because he does not understand all that is said to him. So a child may come to a special class with difficulty in understanding, with poor speech and imperfect English and under some emotional strain because of these difficulties and the misunderstandings they create. Furthermore, a child who has spent some time in an ordinary school before his handicap has been correctly diagnosed may also arrive at the special class with feelings of failure and frustration. Those who have been constant failures are unsure of themselves; those who have received punishment for these failures are embittered; and those who have been neglected because of apparent stupidity are not interested in school work. There may also be in the special class children who have suddenly become deaf through illness and who are suffering from the traumatic effects of this. Rehabilitation for these children should begin at the stage of convalescence and in some instances they can continue to cope in an ordinary class with the part-time assistance of a peripatetic teacher. Some, however, need the full-time help of a special class and they, too, come with their specific problems.

It should be evident that one of the primary tasks of a teacher in a special class is that of rehabilitation or readjustment. The pupils must feel that the teacher understands their problems and their needs and that they are secure in an environment in which they can succeed and progress. Sometimes the mere fact of being placed in a class alongside other pupils similarly handicapped is therapeutic in itself, but frequently a longer period of adjustment and help, in the shape of providing tasks in which success can be easily achieved, is required. Occasionally the problem is very difficult to solve as in the case of M.B. who became profoundly deaf from meningitis at the age of nine. He could not be persuaded to try to lipread. He got virtually no help from a hearing aid and even after two years in a special class could hardly follow anything said by the teacher. His reading was extremely good and he enjoyed reading and could follow any explanations written on the blackboard, but he could not adjust himself to the problems of comprehending speech. Even when motivation seemed to be high, as on the occasion when he asked his mother what was in the case she was carrying and it seemed as if he might make an effort to try to understand what she said, he very quickly gave up and added, "Never mind, I'll find out when we get home."

Dealing with emotional difficulties and establishing a satisfactory means of communication are the first essentials in a special class. The former may not be capable of immediate solution and the latter may well need to be continued for the whole of the time that the pupil is a member of the class. The pupil's own speech will, as noted above, usually require attention in certain respects. This is likely to consist mainly of improving the consonants, in double and triple groups as well as singly. This should mean individual speech lessons and, as with deaf pupils, short daily periods are essential for this purpose. The children will also need to be encouraged and trained to make the best possible use of their residual hearing as a means of understanding the speech of others. For this purpose, a group aid and an inductance loop system (which can be driven from the amplifier of the group aid) are desirable in each special classroom. The group aid should be

M

used for class and small group lessons in which the pupils can reasonably be expected to sit at their desks for the greater part of the time. Where more movement and activity is desirable, the loop system will be used. For individual speech lessons use can either be made of the group aid or alternatively a speech training aid can be provided for this purpose. As will be seen from the sample audiograms shown in Table 9, children will vary very considerably in their ability to discriminate speech through aided hearing. Pupils B.C. and C.B. on that table are likely to be able to discriminate well whilst B.A., B.E. and C.D. will have much more difficulty. B.C. and C.B. can probably hear almost all the sounds of speech when they are amplified and their articulation can be improved to a very large extent through hearing. The others may get only imperfect patterns of many of the consonants and will need visual and other clues to enable them to pronounce the sounds correctly.

Some form of auditory training is also desirable for these pupils so that they can make full use of their hearing. This again is best done on an individual basis, probably at the same time as the speech lesson, and will consist of systematic practice in learning to listen carefully and identify the phrases, words and sounds which are used by the teacher. Some of the games and practices described by Lowell and Stoner (8) are very useful for this purpose. Singing is possible with most of these children and is valuable training in itself as well as providing a form of auditory training. Dramatic work, particularly with puppets, can provide satisfying motivation for good and correct speech.

It is assumed that the special classrooms will be adequately acoustically treated. This will enable the pupils to make the most effective use of their residual hearing. When they are able to take some subjects in ordinary classes they must, of course, learn to adjust to the poorer acoustic conditions to be met with there. This is part of the general process of learning to cope with work in an ordinary class, and is as essential as all other preparations to this end. It is not enough to have reached a standard of work that would make integration possible if the pupil is unable to understand what is said by the teacher in the ordinary classroom. It is possible for the specialist teacher to give some help towards this by, say, utilising for occasional special lesson an ordinary classroom which had been temporarily vacated by its usual class. At a time when the less advanced pupils were taking physical education or handwork with the hearing pupils two or three more advanced pupils could have a lesson in the untreated room using their wearable aids only. At first these lessons would have to be repetitions of fairly familiar material so that the pupils would not experience much difficulty in following the teacher. Later lessons would involve presentation of new material and the pupils' capacity to follow these would have to be taken into account in deciding on the possibility of integrating them for certain subjects into an ordinary class.

Communication has been stressed, since the more rapidly the pupils learn to express themselves clearly and understand the teacher thoroughly, the sooner will they be able to tackle ordinary school subjects. The actual content of the curriculum, in terms of activities and subjects, will approximate to that for hearing pupils at the same stage—infant or junior. Reading is particularly important for it is only through reading that complete patterns of words and phrases will become apparent. It is therefore important in such classes that, particularly at the infant and lower junior stages, much time is devoted to developing reading skills. Once a modicum of this has been attained the children should be led on to express themselves in writing—a skill that many of these pupils find quite difficult, largely because of the imperfect patterns of speech which they receive. The reading books used in the special class should be the same as those used in the ordinary classes. More supplementary readers may be required at each stage and progress through them may be slower but if the pupils are to join the ordinary classes at some stage in their school lives it is essential that they should have covered the same ground.

At the infant stage it is probably desirable that the children should spend the full school day in the special class. At the junior stage, however, the pupils should be attached to normal classes for physical education, art and handwork at least. As pupils become more and more proficient in communication and as their attainments in certain subjects reach a level at which they could benefit from attending their ordinary class for one or more subjects, they should be allowed to do so for these lessons also.

What was said above about reading books is also applicable to other textbooks used in the school. Pupils may take longer to get through them and will probably need more help in working with them than their normally hearing peers but they need a similar background of knowledge if they are going to join them for some, if not all, subjects. This is equally true of the content of the whole curriculum at the junior stage. It should be basically the same as for the junior department of the hearing school, although the pupils in the special class will take longer to cover it, in most cases. Additionally, of course, the partially hearing pupils will have their special lessons in speaking and listening, mainly on an individual basis.

It was stated in Chapter 3 that the primary aim of the special class or unit was to help the partially hearing child to 'integrate' either wholly or partly into a normal hearing class. The length of time that will be required for this to take place will vary from pupil to pupil, but unless there is at least partial integration by the end of the primary stage, the pupil will not have been rightly placed. Partially hearing pupils who require full-time special help for the whole of their school lives should be placed in schools for partially hearing pupils and not in classes or units attached to ordinary schools. The chief reason for attaching such a class to an ordinary school is to enable the pupils to take part in at least some of the school work alongside hearing pupils and if this cannot be done because the pupils are not capable of it then the *raison d'être* of the unit ceases. One is bound to admit that some pupils may not achieve what was expected of them but if the process of regular revision of placement that was recommended is carried out such pupils will be transferred from the special class to a special school.

It has seemed necessary to be quite clear about the function of these classes in order to avoid placing such a heterogeneous mixture of pupils in a class that the teacher's task becomes impossible, to the detriment of those children for whom such a placement would have been appropriate. It took a very long time for it to be recognised that the education of deaf and partially hearing children together was inappropriate and helped neither category. These proposals are intended to prevent it from being as long again before it is also recognised that there are wide varieties amongst partially hearing pupils and that they cannot all be appropriately educated with the same kind of arrangements.

Schools for Partially Hearing Pupils

It would appear that schools for the partially hearing have generally to cater for two types of pupils. One group consists of the children who might be described as 'severely partially deaf', whose handicap has been ascertained at an early age and whose parents have been given guidance during the pre-school years. Their linguistic development is proceeding 'along normal lines', but, because of the severity of their hearing losses, it is restricted. They are rightly placed in a school for the partially hearing because they can gain much of their education through their hearing although this will need to be supplemented by lipreading. They will thus be able to extend their knowledge more rapidly than children who are classified as 'deaf'. The other type of pupils is one who has a less severe hearing loss but has been transferred to the special school because of continued failure to make progress in an ordinary school. Educational retardation, speech defects and communication difficulties all make full-time special educational treatment essential. In addition, there are likely to be emotional problems brought about by failure in the previous school environment.

It might appear that this second group differs very little from that described in special class or unit placement. In some cases this will be true, since pupils from less populous areas, where it is not possible to provide classes attached to ordinary schools for lack of numbers, will of necessity have to attend special schools. However, there are other cases where, at the time of diagnosis, because, for example, of lack of intellectual ability or of deterioration in hearing, it seems likely that the pupils will require full-time special education either for the whole of their school lives or at least for the next few years.

These two types of pupils have different needs and the education provided will obviously have to follow different lines. It thus seems likely that special schools for partially hearing pupils require to be organised on a two-stream basis to cater for these two types of pupils. Of course, if it is possible, pupils will be transferred from such a special school to a unit or even an ordinary school if they are able to fit into these environments at a later stage, but it will generally be expected that the pupils enrolled in the school are likely to spend the whole of their school lives there. This being so, the aim for both types of pupils will be to develop their abilities to the highest possible level with a view perhaps to transferring them to the grammar school for deaf and partially hearing pupils and certainly to following a secondary course which may lead to some type of leaving certificate at its termination.

The first group mentioned, consisting of the children with greater hearing losses, will at first need to follow a curriculum which passes through the same stages as the curriculum outlined for deaf children, but, of course, the stages should be achieved more rapidly. Those who are not already doing so on admission will need to learn to talk in sentences, their vocabulary will have to be extended, their speech improved and their skill in following the speech of others developed. Lessons involving directed activities and stories will help towards the achievement of most of these aims, so that by the time the pupils leave the infant stage they should be capable of following simple lessons and taking part in activities comparable with those found in ordinary junior schools. The pace will be slower than that of the pupils in the units but the pattern need not vary very greatly. Group and individual speech and hearing lessons will be extremely important at the infant and junior stages. Although the children will have a considerable amount of useful hearing, there are likely to be many sounds or combinations of sounds which they are unable to hear correctly or at all, and which will have to be developed through the visual and tactile techniques that have been devised for use with profoundly deaf children. Nevertheless, much of the speech improvement can take place through hearing and the use of speech training aids for individual speech improvement is strongly to be recommended. Group aids and loop systems will be used for other lessons and activities and some time should be spent on helping the pupils to develop to as great a degree as possible their residual hearing. Some of the activities mentioned previously (p. 178) would be appropriate for this purpose. In order to ensure that pupils have the best opportunity for using hearing aids, adequate acoustic treatment of class and other rooms is essential.

Reading and writing are basic skills that must be developed for the same reasons as were given when discussing them for children in special classes. For the rest of the junior school programme the curriculum of the ordinary junior school should be followed as far as possible whilst recognising that these pupils are likely to be working at a level one, or perhaps two, years behind their hearing contemporaries.

At the senior stage, it is probably best to regroup the two types of pupils in a different way. There will still have to be two streams but the streams will now be organised according to ability so that both may contain pupils from each of the two original groups who have shown that they are capable of working at a slower or a faster pace, as the case may be. The abler groups may be expected to work for G.C.E. in certain subjects, or for the Certificate of Secondary Education; some of the less able group may find it possible to aim at the Certificate of Secondary Education in one or two subjects. Those working for G.C.E. will, of course, have to follow an appropriate curriculum, although each school is likely to be rather limited in the number of subjects for which adequate provision can be made. Those working for C.S.E., or without the expectation of a leaving certificate, should follow courses something like those described above for deaf children at the secondary stage. They will, of course, be expected to take courses with a largely verbal content to a higher level than most of the severely deaf pupils.

Such proposals presuppose, as in the case of schools for deaf children, that there are members of staff suitably qualified to teach these courses and that the school has adequate classroom and laboratory facilities to enable the subjects to be properly taught and studied.

For the second type of pupil at the primary stage there is need, as was suggested for pupils in units, for a period of readjustment. They are coming to the special school as failures and their first need is to be shown that they can achieve successfully the tasks set in their new environment. Unless they have confidence in their ability to succeed, little progress is likely to be made. Those pupils whose hearing loss is of long standing but who are intellectually of below average standard are likely to have some articulatory errors in their speech, but although these need attention and improvement, speech is not a major problem. Those who have been deafened after the acquisition of normal speech must have a close watch kept on their speech in order to prevent any deterioration from taking place. If the deafness is very severe, as it frequently is after, for example, meningitis, they may be unable to hear the sound of their own voices and thus monitor their speech. Without a careful check being kept on the slightest signs of regression and steps being taken to counteract this there is a very considerable risk of a perhaps imperceptible but serious deterioration in their speech. It is tragic to hear, as one has done, a pupil of sixteen years of age with virtually unintelligible speech who had normal speech up to the age of seven years when she became profoundly deaf. Such a tragedy is, unfortunately, not unique.

In addition to this attention to speech conservation, it is common to find that pupils whose hearing is deteriorating need special help to enable them to understand the speech of others. Help in making the fullest use of their residual hearing is important but perhaps even more important for these children is help in acquiring some skill in lipreading. At the primary stage this would not involve formal training in recognising the different shapes of the lips and visible tongue positions but rather practice, at first, in very clear-cut situations gradually leading up to the development of comprehension with very limited clues save the verbal ones. The written work of children with partial hearing losses of long standing has often been observed to be exceptionally poor in comparison with their spoken language. This is understandable in view of the very incomplete patterns which they receive, but it also seems to indicate that not enough stress has been laid upon the development of reading skills. Careful and systematic training in reading will enable the pupils to fill in the gaps of the imperfect heard/seen patterns and also give them correct patterns to be utilised in written work. The content of the curriculum for these children at the primary stage should be modelled on that for ordinary hearing pupils. The pace will be slower and the rate of progress may be less, so that like the other group described above, they will probably still be retarded educationally by the time they reach secondary school age. It is likely, too, that in view of variations in hearing loss, ability and even age, in these classes, it will be desirable to work in small groups within the class. In this way the needs of individual pupils can more readily be catered for and each can be enabled to work at the pace of which he is capable. Although not particularly directed to children with this type of handicap there are some useful suggestions on curriculum content and methods in the Cheshire Education Committee's book entitled *The Education of Dull Children at the Primary Stage* (9).

It has already been proposed that pupils in this category should be considered with the deafer group to form two differently organised streams at the secondary stage.

It must also be borne in mind that the original placement may have been mistaken or that some pupils have made such progress as would warrant a reassessment of placement. Consequently some pupils allocated to full-time education in a special school may be found likely to benefit from a transfer to an ordinary school or a unit. Such a transfer, however, should not be considered without the special school being satisfied that the pupil is capable of coping with the change and without those responsible for making the transfer being sure that the receiving school or class is fully aware of and prepared to help with the problems that such a child will have on transfer. In a report by Miss E. M. Johnson, published by the Ministry of Education (10), some of the difficulties and dangers of making such transfers are described. It is true that most difficulties arose in the case of deaf pupils but of the fourteen partially hearing children considered in the report only in six cases had the transfers been clearly successful. In a further six cases they had been moderately successful and in two cases failures. Despite this, the survey made it clear that a very large number of conditions had to be satisfied before there was a likelihood of success.

It may be felt that the suggestions made with regard to curriculum and levels of attainment of these partially hearing pupils expect too much from them. In defence of the suggestions it is believed that the level of aspiration for the pupils needs to be high. There is a risk that specialist teachers with a single course of training to qualify them as teachers of the deaf and partially hearing may not sufficiently distinguish between the needs and capabilities of the two groups. This is no argument for separating the courses of training: on the contrary it seems that the integration is in the best interests of both pupils and teachers. However, it must be pointed out that although actual methods of teaching will differ from one type of pupil to the other, the attainments that can be expected of partially hearing children should be greater and the rate at which they can be achieved should be faster. A special school is a school in which special methods are used but not necessarily one in which lower terminal standards are expected as a matter of course. The nature and extent of the disability may preclude the achievement of normal standards, but the pupils need to be given the opportunity of learning up to the maximum of their capacities and, in at least some cases, this may be little if anything below that of non-handicapped pupils.

REFERENCES

1 Johnson, J. C. (1962). *Educating Hearing Impaired Children in Ordinary Schools*. Manchester Univ. Press

2 Brereton, B. Le G. (1957). *The Schooling of Children with Impaired Hearing.* Commonwealth Office of Education, Sydney, Australia

3 Goetzinger, C. P. (1962). 'Effects of Small Perceptive Losses on Language and on Speech Discrimination'. *Volta Review,* 64, 408

4 Kodman, F. (1963). 'Educational Status of Hard of Hearing Children in the Classroom'. *J. of Sp. and Hearing Dis.* 28, 297

5 Sanders, D. A. (1961). *A Follow-up Study of Fifty Children who received Pre-School Training.* Unpublished Ph.D. thesis, Univ. of Manchester Library

6 Mutch, D. C. (1964). *The Oral and Written Expression of Children with Impaired Hearing and Unimpaired Hearing in a Secondary Modern School.* Thesis in preparation for the degree of M.Ed. Manchester Univ.

7 Warfield, F. (1949). *There's No Need to Shout.* Gollancz

8 Lowell, E. & Stoner, M. (1960). *Play it by Ear.* John Tracy Clinic, Los Angeles

9 Cheshire Education Committee (1956). *The Education of Dull Children at the Primary Stage.* Univ. of London Press Ltd.

10 Ministry of Education (1963). *A Report on a Survey of Deaf Children.* HMSO

7

Parental co-operation

The more one meets deaf pupils who have achieved high standards, socially as well as educationally, the more it becomes clear that a decisive influence in their progress has been the help given to them by their parents. The short biographies of deaf children written by their parents in Chapter IX of *New Opportunities for Deaf Children*; the account of her daughter's development by Mrs Freddie Bloom in *Our Deaf Children*; and numerous brief biographical snatches in the Parents' Section of the *Volta Review*, serve as further witnesses to the importance of this influence. A quarter of a century ago the attitude in many of the schools was 'leave it to us'; some even went further as, for example, the headmaster of a school for the deaf who refused to allow parents to come beyond the front door of the school since he believed that they were at best 'a necessary evil'!

The climate of opinion in this, as in many other matters, has fortunately changed and it is becoming increasingly recognised that co-operation between school and parents is vital to the optimum development of the child. Indeed, not only is school/parental co-operation important but the parents have an essential part to play themselves in the overall development of their children. Not only cannot the school do it alone, but the school cannot do at all many of the things which parents can and must do if their child is to become a well adjusted, mature and well educated adult.

There is already a considerable amount of information about ways in which parents can help their children at the pre-school stage (1, 2, 3, 4). This pre-school training is essential to help the child develop intellectually, emotionally and socially before he is ready to go to school and its importance has been recognised by the Department of Education and Science, the Ministry of Health and by local authorities who have appointed peripatetic teachers to give guidance to the parents and have set up clinics to ascertain deafness at as early an age as possible. Since this book is concerned mainly with children at school it is not proposed to deal with pre-school children any further and in any case a considerable amount of material on this topic is now available. It does, however, seem useful to discuss the kind of help that parents need to give to their children whilst they are pupils at school and this may serve as a complement and a supplement to what has already been said about education in previous chapters. It would seem useful to outline what can and should be done under two main heads—what the parents do in the home, and what parent/teacher co-operation involves. The two will obviously overlap because the function of the latter is largely to assist parents in the execution of the former.

THE ROLE OF THE FAMILY IN EDUCATION

Almost all proposals for the guidance of parents of deaf children at the pre-school stage draw attention to the need for acceptance of their child's handicap on the part of parents. This is the firm base on which the whole edifice of training and help stands; without it, nothing worthwhile or lasting can develop. This is just as true when the child is of school age as it was earlier, and in order to make a success of their efforts, parents must accept their handicapped child as he is. This means that time is not wasted trying to find cures and explanations for the cause of deafness and that the child is not overprotected because of his disability nor rejected because the parents have a guilt feeling or cannot bring themselves to make the effort to help. By treating their child as a normal member of the family, by ensuring that he participates in family life in the same measure that he would have done were he not deaf, and by imaginatively and constructively assisting in his development, parents will be providing the kind of home background which nurtures security and growth. Four short quotations from the well-known American writer on child care, Dr Spock (5), summarise this attitude well:

Parents can do their best by a handicapped child if they are able to think of him, feel toward him, care for him as a child who in most respects is like other children, with the same needs and responses. . . .

Overconcern is unwholesome for him, for his brothers and sisters and for his parents. Its only use, really, is as a tranquillizer for the parents' uneasiness. . . .

If the parents can act as if the handicapped child were a regular child except for the defect, love him, enjoy him, expect his best efforts, require his cooperation, punish when punishment is due, feel no great embarrassment about him, the other children will tend to accept him on the same basis. . . .

It's good for brothers and sisters to see that the handicapped child is expected to conform, be polite, be generous, be helpful. It's even more important for the child himself. This is what really convinces him that he's a regular member of the family. . . .

In making suggestions for ways in which parents can provide help, it will be assumed that they have already had some information and guidance during the pre-school years. They will therefore be aware of the extent of their child's hearing loss and know to what degree he can be helped by the use of a hearing aid. They will also know how he can be helped to lipread and understand through guidance in specific situations, and how he can be encouraged to use his voice as a means of communicating with others. The correct volume setting of the hearing aid will have been explained and also the importance of speech close to the microphone both by parents and child so that the latter can hear his own vocalisations and begin to match them to the speech of his parents. Some parents may indeed have fixed up an inductance loop in the home so that the child may be in closer contact with them wherever he or they may be in the house.

Parents who have not had this help during the pre-school years should be given it when the child begins to attend school so that they are aware of the basis on which communication can be developed in the home. Upon this basis there are a great many ways in which linguistic development can be encouraged.

Perhaps the most important contribution that parents can make is the encouragement that they give their child to talk. In every situation in which speech would be expected from a hearing child it should be expected from a deaf child. In the early stages the speech may be largely unintelligible and the phrase or sentence may be only one word in length, but the important thing is to establish the principle of talking. Gestures will have to be accepted for unknown vocabulary but when made by the child they should be instantly translated into words by the parents and the child encouraged to repeat the words. A child should not be allowed to gesture for something when it is certain that he knows the words. As he grows older colloquial words and phrases should be given to the child at the appropriate times and after they have occurred many times in similar situations he should be expected to use them. At first these are the more obvious ones such as 'please', 'thank you', or 'hello'. Later he needs to learn phrases such as 'Excuse me', 'Pass the . . ., please' and 'May I . . .'. These and many other similar phrases are, or should be, routine in the home and normal life should provide plenty of opportunities for practice. Some or most of these phrases will probably have been taught and used in school, but the situations in which they occur in the home may well be different and in any case the opportunities for their use are likely to be much greater than at school. In addition to this conversational use of language, it will be necessary to help the child to extend his vocabulary of things in the home environment. This would include the kinds of foods served; the utensils used in cooking; the names of special pieces of furniture or equipment and their uses; garden tools; the names of neighbours, shops and streets in the vicinity of the home. This vocabulary should not, of course, be given by the parents as lists of words, but when the name comes up appropriately as, for example, when meeting a neighbour in the street or preparing a meal, the parent should give the child the best opportunity for learning the new word through his hearing and lipreading. When the child is able to read, the new words may be written down later in the day. Opportunity should be given for the revision which is necessary to help the child to remember the words—when Father comes home he could be told whom they met in the street, or when sitting at table the child could be asked to tell the other members of the family what was used in the preparation of the meal. In imaginative ways, such as these, it is possible to provide many opportunities for talking, for practising new words and phrases and for showing the child that he is an integral part of the family.

Another way of encouraging talking and extending and using vocabulary lies in the teaching of the words and phrases used in outdoor and indoor games. This will help the child greatly in his play with other children and the use of the right phrases at the appropriate times will not only give the child the practice he needs in communication but will prevent him from appearing stupid in the eyes of his hearing playmates.

Opportunities for parents to widen their child's knowledge also come through the provision of interesting experiences outside the home which have been adequately prepared for. The obvious examples that spring to mind are visits to the zoo, the docks or the airport, to a museum to see some particular exhibits or some expedition related to the particular interests of the child. To be of real value there must be careful preparation:

for example, if it is a visit to the zoo that is being planned an explanation should be given of how the family will travel, some of the animals that may be seen, possibly looking at picture books which illustrate them, where the meal will be eaten if away from home and, if it is to be a picnic, the child could be given the opportunity of helping with the preparations. After the visit is over, but not necessarily on the same day, it would be useful to contrive that a relative or visitor should call and, without its appearing to be too obviously arranged, the child should be encouraged to describe as well as possible what was seen and done.

When the child has learned to read, the home has a considerable part to play in the encouragement of this skill. The provision of a shelf on the bookcase for the child's own books, visits to the local library to select a book and the evident enjoyment of parents in reading are all ways in which an interest in books can be stimulated. Parents can also tell the child something about the books and magazine or newspaper articles they are reading and expect the child to tell them a little of the content of their own books. Reading for information can be developed through encouragement of hobbies. The child who collects cigarette cards can be expected to read and retail some of the information contained on the reverse side. Boys who are interested in trains or cars or stamps can be encouraged to look up pieces of information from books. They can also learn simple conjuring tricks and experiments. Girls can look up and follow recipes or directions for making garments or learn about dolls from other countries or any other subjects which may interest them. The use of a 'bulletin board' in the home can also serve as an encouragement to reading. It can contain pieces of information such as 'We are going to tea at Mrs Brown's on Sunday afternoon', or a list of duties expected from the child during the week, or messages, or the occasional captioned picture or cartoon. There are, of course, many other ways of encouraging reading that can be devised by parents who choose to use their ingenuity—from the keeping of picture dictionaries at an earlier stage to the keeping of diaries by teenagers.

When the children are older juniors, parents can help them to improve their use of language by encouraging the use of correct patterns. Parents will listen to what their child has to say and then, where necessary, suggest appropriate corrections. As far as possible the child should be expected to think out the right construction himself. Phrases such as 'Now can you say that better', or 'Remember how I told you to say that' should become familiar to the child and he should try to express his thoughts more conventionally. Sometimes, a simple reminder such as 'You forgot...', or 'You didn't say...' will be all that is necessary to evoke a better pattern. In the same way, without necessarily feeling that they must teach their children to improve their pronunciation, a matter which is best left to the professional skill of the teacher, parents can encourage them to say words as well as they know how—to put in the 's' sound, for example, or say 'Monday' instead of 'Mboniday'. It is here, as well as in many other facets of the communication between home and school, that the home/school notebook referred to in Chapter 5 is extremely useful. From it the parents will find out which sounds the child can say correctly and which he has not yet mastered. They will also be able to let the teacher know some of the phrases which they are encouraging the child to use at home so that the teacher may be able to include these in her speech improvement lessons.

We have been concerned so far with the linguistic development of the child and ways in which parents can contribute to this. There are, of course, many other aspects of development about which parents are deeply concerned and, in some ways, must take even more responsibility for than the school does. Some of these relate to behaviour. Many patterns of behaviour in childhood are developed through verbal communication: 'Don't hold your spoon that way', 'Stop . . .', 'It's Mary's turn to ride in the truck now'. These and hosts of other commands, instructions and prohibitions which are given in trying to develop the modes of behaviour desired by the parents depend, to a very large extent, upon an understanding of language. This, of course, is another reason for the necessity of trying to develop language as a means of communication early in life so that the right behaviour habits can be instilled as soon as possible. Whilst help about social training and behaviour will have been given to the parents during their child's pre-school years, there is still a need for this training to continue whilst the child is at school. Example here is at least as good as precept and parents must not have a dual standard—one for adults and another for their children. Thus, manners and the outward social graces should be copied from parents' behaviour just as much as the instructions and explanations should be given verbally. Such of these as are necessary must obviously be very simple and at a language level at which they are likely to be understood.

Interwoven with the child's attitude towards others is his attitude towards himself—the development of his own view of his personality. This comes, as Spock again points out, "primarily from the way his parents view him. Whether they consider him weak or husky, attractive or unappealing, good or bad, pathetic or terrific, he will tend—other things being equal—to accept their view." This is perhaps an oversimplification of the development of consciousness of self, but it is important inasmuch as it underlines the significance of parental attitudes in helping the child to come to terms with himself.

Along with social behaviour is included moral behaviour and attitudes. Truthfulness, honesty, unselfishness, kindness and the like may not be easily understood in the abstract but they can be developed in real-life situations. Indeed, many people when asked to define those terms do so by means of examples. Insistence upon high standards and the use of clear situations whenever possible to illustrate these standards seem to be the best ways of helping to develop an acceptable moral code. Of course, the more that the ideas can be framed in language understood by the child the greater is the likelihood of their having a significant and lasting impact. So much of what a hearing child learns of the behaviour and attitudes of other people is based upon what he hears and overhears of their conversations. He develops a social awareness which may well colour his own behaviour and attitudes. The deaf child misses this and the result is not only an inability to set up personal standards without help but also a naïveté about the standards of his native culture. Parents therefore must stand not only as exemplars but also as interpreters of the world outside the home. It was pointed out in Chapter 5 that a sign of increasing maturity was concern for others. There is a considerable risk that without a great deal of help many deaf children may not acquire this and may become quite self-centred and oblivious to the needs of others. In order to try to meet this problem the National Deaf Children's Society established a National League of Service to attempt to make deaf children aware of others. It has not, so far, been an unqualified success but it is a brave attempt to fill a gap in the development of greater

N

maturity and there is a likelihood that it may be more successful in the near future. Parents who themselves have a Christian faith will wish their children to acquire it also. To a very large extent, Christian teaching in the home will follow the pattern of that for hearing children. Simple prayers will be taught and learned, the salient points of denominational worship explained simply in relation to the maturity and linguistic development of the child, and Christian behaviour and attitudes practised in the home and demonstrated by example. To supplement the religious teaching of the school use can be made, during a short Sunday story-time, for example, of a Bible picture book. When a child has the ability to read the stories he could do this aloud and have questions and explanations about them from the parents, or better still the story illustrated by a picture could be told by the parent to the child. Here again, it is important for the parents to be prepared to answer children's questions as honestly as they can, having regard to the linguistic skill and level of understanding of the child. Sunday-school attendance, which is suggested later, might well be considered to be practicable if adequate preparations are made. There could be many advantages gained from this in terms of social and linguistic development as well as religious observation and education.

The need for parents to act as interpreters of the world is particularly true when a child is growing up into adolescence. There are the physical signs of growth to be dealt with as well as the psychological problems that accompany them. Whilst it is true that the process of growing up involves a lessening of parental influence and a striving for independence, yet the home has of necessity a great deal to give to a deaf child at this stage. The school can probably deal with some of the biological and physiological information that is part of sex education but, for example, the changes that occur at puberty and the facts of procreation and childbirth are matters that are more suitably discussed by the parents. Of course, some of this information need not wait until the onset of adolescence—questions about where babies come from, and such like, should be dealt with as they arise, usually at a much earlier stage, and should be answered honestly but only at the level at which the child is capable of understanding. Such factual matters are not too difficult to deal with but a much more difficult task that the parent has to face is trying to explain sexual relationships satisfactorily. Many parents may feel embarrassed at having to express openly their views on such a subject, but unless deaf adolescents are given guidance in what parents believe to be right behaviour, it is difficult to see how a satisfactory adult life can ensue for them. They may, moreover, in their naïveté, be susceptible to the influences of adventurers of both sexes. Parents, of course, are unlikely to be able to help here unless they have previously established an easy relationship with their children and a ready means of communication. There must already be an understanding that all questions will be answered and the honesty of the parents' answers should never be in doubt. This, of course, is true with all children but it is especially so in the case of children who are deaf.

Another matter which is not specifically concerned with linguistic development is the help and encouragement which can be given to the child to develop interesting leisure-time pursuits. Many of these, at the primary stage, are, of course, ephemeral interests, but this is the normal pattern of the stage of development and they should not be discouraged. Collecting a variety of objects, drawing and painting, model railways, somewhat grandiose plans for models in cardboard and wood, construction of shelters and dens in the garden: all these and many others can be turned to advantage in the development of language and as a basis for communication, but at the same time they can lay the foundations for more lasting interests and hobbies. Interest in them can be used to encourage reading, as was noted above, by searching for appropriate books in a library. At a later stage, the child's interests will tend to crystallise in one or two well-defined channels and this should be encouraged as providing an outlet for the creative urge and a satisfying way of using leisure time which gives relief from the strain of communicating with others. Whilst not actually engaged in the leisure-time pursuit, it can constitute a useful means of contact and subject of conversation with others.

In addition to helping linguistic development, taking responsibility for promoting acceptable behaviour patterns and encouraging leisure-time pursuits, parents can also assist by helping children in their relationships with other children, particularly the hearing children with whom they are likely to come into contact in the community in which the family lives. A deaf or even a partially hearing child can be an embarrassment as a playmate to normal hearing children unless they are made aware of the difficulties of the child. A hearing-handicapped child who is rejected or ignored by his hearing peers will withdraw into his own little world and will not easily adjust to hearing society when he grows up. From the outset, therefore, it is necessary for parents to encourage the development of good social relations with hearing children in the neighbourhood. The hearing children need to have explained to them the fact that the hearing-handicapped child cannot hear, or only hear imperfectly; that consequently his speech is not as good as theirs; and that he will frequently have difficulty in understanding new ideas. When children are aware of these matters, it is usually surprising what efforts they will make to help out the hearing-handicapped child. At the same time, parents must help their hearing-handicapped child by making sure, for example, that he knows the names of his play-mates and where they live, that he understands the rules of the games that are usually played and also some of the terms commonly used in these games. This was suggested earlier as one of the ways in which language development could be encouraged. Parents, therefore, need to keep abreast of the current popular games and up to date with the jargon and catch-phrases used in them. If there are hearing siblings in the family this makes the parents' task easier, but it is quite essential that the handicapped child should be helped to acquire this information.

Allied to this matter is the question of whether or not the child should be encouraged to join organisations alongside hearing children. Such organisations would include Cubs and Scouts, Brownies and Guides, youth clubs, sports clubs, etc.: it could also include Sunday-schools. With the kind of preparation suggested above for the receiving organisation and the support for the hearing-handicapped child at home, association with such organisations can be extremely valuable and should be encouraged whenever possible.

In the suggestions given above, which are by no means exhaustive, no distinction has been drawn with regard to the child's attendance at school as a day pupil or as a boarder. Obviously this matter will have a bearing on the extent to which parents can contribute towards his general development. However, the effect will be on the extent rather than the kind of help that can be given. It is true that the suggestions have been put forward with the day school pupils mainly in mind, but they are equally relevant to the times that the boarding school pupil spends at home—week-ends, holidays etc. Indeed, an American teacher has written that "it is an ill-advised parent who thinks that the child home from a residential school is simply on vacation and need not be held to some sort of disciplinary learning" (6). A deaf adult has confessed how much she owes to the fact that her mother insisted that she wrote a short composition every morning during her summer holidays. This latter is perhaps an extreme case of parental concern but it illustrates the significance of parental influence and encouragement. In the case of a young hearing child, language acquisition goes on all the time: if the child's opportunities for this stop at the end of the school day or when he comes home on holiday then his language will be all the poorer and his capacity for development in a variety of ways stunted.

This, of course, all adds up to a great deal of time and thought being expended by the parents of a hearing-handicapped child. Having a handicapped child, however, is a challenge to the parents and the way in which they meet this challenge is a measure of themselves as mature people. Having other siblings to care for is not entirely a valid excuse for limiting the help, for the other children can assist in the handicapped child's development— as for example, the little hearing girl of seven who was seen to use a speech training aid most effectively to talk to and encourage the talking by her severely deaf sister of three. As Mrs Bloom has said (7), "the bigger the family the more the handicap can be shared". At any rate, it does seem apparent that without this active participation by parents in the whole development of their hearing-handicapped children the latter will not achieve the standards of which they are capable and to which legitimate aspirations would lead.

PARENT/TEACHER CO-OPERATION

Parents, however, should not be expected to cope with their problems unsupported and without guidance. When a child attends a special class or school he ceases to be the responsibility of the guidance clinic although obviously much of the advice and help received by the parents in the pre-school years is relevant to later stages. Responsibility for helping the parents now passes over to the school and it is in this context that parent/teacher associations are essential. This is hardly the place to discuss the organisation of such an association but some suggestions of the kind of activities that might be followed may be appropriate.

In the first place, one of the functions of the association is to give information to the parents. This means that talks, films and demonstrations should be arranged to present specific pieces of information. For example, a series of talks might be devoted to the topic Hearing. These would seek to explain in simple terms the mechanism of hearing, the effects of deafness of different types and etiologies, how hearing is measured, and so forth. Another series could describe the different kinds of hearing aids, how to make the most effective use of aids, care of individual aids etc. Yet other series could deal in the same way with Speech, Understanding the Speech of Deaf Pupils, Helping Your Child to Improve his English, The Encouragement of Reading and so on in an almost unlimited list. The series would vary in length, but the main object would be to clarify in the parents' minds the effects of deafness and ways in which it can be alleviated. Wherever possible, points would be demonstrated and there should be opportunities for parents to ask questions for clarification. The object of these factual talks would not be to help a particular parent with his own problems: they would be too general for that. They would, however, give parents basic information which they could relate to their own problems. Help to individual parents will be discussed a little later.

It might be useful to have the main facts of these talks duplicated or printed so that they could be sent to all parents to increase their knowledge of deafness and its associated problems. In fact, a series of pamphlets on the above lines could well be issued by a national organisation and distributed by schools to the parents of every child enrolled. If this were done they could form the bases for discussions at parent/teacher association meetings but they should not be allowed to take the place of such meetings.

Another way of providing information for parents and keeping them in touch with developments in the school and the educational world in general is by means of a news letter. The parent/teacher association of one well-known school in the United States issues such a letter monthly except during the summer vacation. It is duplicated and contains from twenty-four to thirty-two quarto pages. The contents are typically an editorial, an article by a member of staff or reprinted from another source, suggestions for helping parents from teachers in training, reviews of books suitable for parents and those suitable for their children, an occasional article by a senior pupil, special school notes and reports of P.T.A. meetings. The editor in this instance is a parent.

Yet another possible way of disseminating information and keeping parents abreast of developments is an annual one-day conference, with some outside speakers to read short papers and answer questions on their own fields of knowledge.

The second major function of the association is to enable parents to get special help about their own problems and advice about the ways in which they can best help their own children when they are at home. This must be done on an individual basis and is generally best done through consultation with the class teacher. In nursery and infant departments it is often possible to allow parents to 'sit in' for some periods, perhaps once a month or even more frequently. This gives them the opportunity to see how their own children are progressing and ways in which the teacher strives to help them. Such visits also give them an opportunity to consult with the teacher (after school and by appointment) concerning their own contribution to development. It is normally less easy to arrange for this to be done in primary classes but it should be considered not only possible but desirable and necessary that parents should make appointments to see the class teacher not less than once per term. Indeed, if pupils attend the school daily, it is even better for the school to send out notices of appointment to parents once a term to enable the teacher and parent to discuss, at mutually convenient times, the child's needs and problems. Such meetings provide for a two-way exchange of information: not only does the parent get help from the teacher, but what the parent can tell her of the child's interests, attitudes towards others and general behaviour in the home, can be of immense value to the teacher in planning her approach to the whole educational development of the child.

It may be argued that some teachers are too inexperienced to be entrusted with this responsibility. None the less they should be expected to take part in this exchange of information for they have some valuable knowledge of the child's behaviour and progress in school to pass on to the parent and they will benefit greatly from what the parent can tell of the child at home. However, to provide more mature and experienced counsel, a senior teacher ought also to be present at the interview. There is a very strong case in favour of giving a senior teacher at each of the three stages—infant, junior and senior—some special responsibility for parent guidance. Such a teacher would be able to suggest to parents where they could find further information and would be able to utilise the class teacher's knowledge of the child to make suggestions to the parent about the help that could be given at home. This specialist would be well fitted to give answers to problems as a result of his or her wide experience and generally turn the discussion into a valuable experience both for parent and young teacher. Furthermore, the continuity of advice given in this way and the co-ordination of the efforts of parents and teachers at each stage of the child's school career would add immeasurably to his chances of successful development.

This chapter ends, as it began, with an insistence on the need for the parent's role in the education of hearing-handicapped children to be greatly increased. It is not suggested that the parent should become a quasi-teacher or propose to the school how his child should be educated. There could be no argument in favour of parents 'interfering' in the work of the school, for teaching deaf children requires a very high degree of professional skill, but there is a very sound case for ensuring that their work is complementary. It would be pessimistic to suggest that levels of achievement of pupils in schools for the deaf and partially hearing will not rise in the future, but there are strong grounds for believing that they will not rise to the height of which the children are capable without the close co-operation of parents and teachers in a determined drive to bring this about.

REFERENCES

1 Ewing, I. R. & A. W. G. (1961). *New Opportunities for Deaf Children.* University of London Press

2 Harris, Grace M. (1963). *Language for the Pre-School Deaf Child.* Grune & Stratton, New York.

3 Harris, Grace M. (1964). 'For Parents of Very Young Deaf Children'. *Volta Review,* Vol. 66, 19

4 Correspondence Course. John Tracy Clinic, Los Angeles

5 Spock, Benjamin (1961). *On Being the Parent of a Handicapped Child.* National Soc. for Crippled Children & Adults Inc., Chicago

6 Mannen, Grace (1961). 'Enriching the Language of the Older Deaf Child'. *Volta Review,* Vol. 63, 224

7 Bloom, Freddy (1963). *Our Deaf Children.* Heinemann

APPENDIXES

Manchester picture vocabulary test[*]

USE OF TEST

This is a test of speech discrimination or intelligibility. It does not supersede other monosyllabic word list material, but is intended to be used with children whose vocabularies are restricted because of retarded linguistic development and/or whose speech is not readily intelligible. If children are able to discriminate speech sufficiently well to score significantly on Manchester M.J. or other monosyllabic word lists, these should be used in preference to the Picture Vocabulary Test.[†]

The test may be administered through a speech audiometer or a speech training hearing aid. In the latter case the thresholds of detectability for voice of the subjects should be greater than 70 decibels. It is desirable that the audiometer or hearing aid should be calibrated to British Standard zero reference level.

TEST MATERIAL

The test consists of six lists of twenty monosyllabic words each. The vocabulary range is simple and an attempt has been made, within the length of the lists, to secure homogeneity and equality of difficulty. It was not possible to construct them with phonetic balance, but the words were chosen to give as wide a selection as possible of the phonemes in Standard English.

The words are depicted on three sets of twenty cards each. On each card are six pictures, one of which illustrates the stimulus word. A varying number of the other five words contain the same vowels or the same consonants. The tests are mainly of

---

[*] Sets of the picture material needed for administering the Picture Vocabulary Test may be obtained from the Department of Audiology and Education of the Deaf, The University, Manchester, 13.

[†] See Ewing, A. W. G. et al., *Educational Guidance and the Deaf Child* (1957), Chapter 12.

vowel discrimination although, in some cases, to provide 'head room' for children with more hearing, consonant discrimination is tested.

The sets of cards are lettered A, B and C. Word lists A1 and A2 are given, using set A; B1 and B2, using set B; and C1 and C2, using set C. Set A is coloured white; Set B, green; and Set C, buff.

PROCEDURE

The card marked PRACTICE is placed before the child. The audiometer or hearing aid receivers are then placed over the child's ears and by means of lipreading and aided hearing the tester asks him to name the pictures. The tester then asks the subject to "Show me the . . . (e.g. SHOP)". When the subject shows, by pointing to the required picture, that he understands the procedure, the tester tells him to do the same with the other cards.

The child is then put in a position where he cannot see the tester. It is expected that thresholds of detectability for voice will already have been established and the first test is normally given at about 30 db above these levels, or at as high a level as the child can comfortably tolerate, whichever is the lesser.

The tester then proceeds to read through one of the lists of words, prefacing each by the phrase "Show me the . . ." and giving sufficient time between each stimulus word to allow the child to select his response, to turn over the used card and expose the next one.

If the tester has an assistant, the latter will act as scorer and may also be responsible for turning over the cards.

It should be made clear that only one stimulus word is given for each card. If the child is uncertain of the word which has been given it should not be repeated, but he should turn over the card in readiness for the next word.

After the test at the first level has been completed, other lists may be used at levels to be determined on the basis of the results of this first list. Thus, if the score is 100 per cent, lower levels may be used to find out the lowest level at which this score can be made. If the score is less than 100 per cent tests will be given at higher (and also lower) levels to determine the level for optimum discrimination.

Speech audiograms may be constructed on the results of several tests.

NOTES

1. The written symbol is given under each picture so that children who can read may use this additional help.

2. With a choice of one picture out of six on each card a chance factor must enter in. This, however, is not considered to be great and is generally less than similar factors in other multiple-choice test items. When the highest score that a child gains at any level is less than four, however, it should not be considered to be significant. It may be due to chance and it must be concluded that the child's ability to discriminate speech is so poor that the test is not appropriate in this case. In such a case a simple test of discrimination of vowels may be attempted.

3. Although the test is used mainly for the purpose of testing auditory discrimination there is no reason why it should not be used for the purpose of testing comprehension by a combination of aided hearing and lipreading, if this is required.

NORMS

The following curve has been constructed from the average scores of children with normal hearing listening to the tests through telephone receivers in a closed-circuit system:

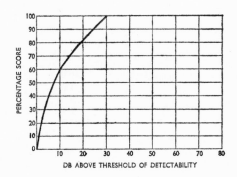

INDIVIDUAL RECORD FORM

Manchester Picture Vocabulary Test
Conditions of test, including loudness level and ear used, to be recorded

Child's Name   *Date of Test*

	List A.1	*List B.1*	*List C.1*
1.	SHIP	BRUSH	GUN
2.	BELL	COAT	KEYS
3.	CHAIR	HEN	STICK
4.	MAN	LID	BOAT
5.	DUCK	KNIFE	SAW
6.	COWS	SNAKE	WHIP
7.	EAR	BALL	SHEEP
8.	BRICKS	TREES	CAKE
9.	SHOES	BOOTS	HOUSE
10.	CLOCK	MILK	DOG
11.	PIPE	GIRL	PEG
12.	CHURCH	STAIRS	BIRD
13.	SOAP	PIG	CAT
14.	WHEEL	LAMB	BOY
15.	PIN	MOUSE	SPOON
16.	BED	SHOP	JAR
17.	LEAVES	CAP	FISH
18.	WALL	CHEESE	MICE
19.	CART	WELL	TAP
20.	BAG	CAR	EGG

	List A.2	*List B.2*	*List C.2*
1.	SHOES	DRUM	MOON
2.	BED	CAT	GIRL
3.	CHEESE	BELL	PIG
4.	CART	MOP	BOWL
5.	BOOK	NAIL	BALL
6.	MOUTH	LAMB	WHEEL
7.	PIN	WALL	SPADE
8.	CHICK	LEAVES	BED
9.	MUG	BOOK	MOUSE
10.	HAND	FISH	DUCK

11.	KITE	PIPE	PAN
12.	LOAF	HOUSE	KNIFE
13.	SOCKS	STICK	MAN
14.	KEYS	MAN	BOX
15.	WHIP	STOOL	WOOL
16.	HEN	CLOCK	CAR
17.	GOAT	TAP	DISH
18.	GIRL	TREES	BEADS
19.	RAKE	PEG	CAP
20.	LAMB	CUP	COWS

Manchester sentence lists

[Only words underlined to be scored]

LIST A
1. The girl's mother has a new red hat.
2. Some people send cards at Easter.
3. Frogs come out of the water to breathe.
4. Mother will bake a cake for my birthday.
5. Indians make birch bark canoes.
6. Some countries have summer in December.
7. Is a twopenny stamp blue or brown?
8. Leave the door key under the mat.
9. Put a tight bandage round his thumb.
10. The first wheels were made from slices of log.

LIST B
1. My friend's father drives a blue car.
2. Would you like some water with your meal?
3. Swallows sometimes fly near the ground.
4. People squeeze lemons to get the juice.
5. The brown deer licked its baby fawn.
6. Stars seem brighter on a dark night.
7. Open your sum book at page fifty-two.
8. School ends at ten past four.
9. Put clean paper on top of the table.
10. The names of some towns end in -ham.

LIST C
1. You can't buy fish in a baker's shop.
2. New shoes are often tiring to wear.
3. Most mice have long thin tails.
4. The shops don't open before eight.

5. People sometimes cross a fence by a stile.
6. Many plants begin to flower in May.
7. The American flag has red and white stripes.
8. Buy some toothpaste in the chemist's shop.
9. Most car engines are cooled by water.
10. Tigers and leopards are members of the cat family.

LIST D

1. Father comes home from work at six.
2. Please sew a button on the vest.
3. The man had cheese and dry biscuits for supper.
4. Fresh water fish are caught with flies.
5. We do not often have snow in September.
6. Many women use gas for cooking.
7. Bears often sleep on the branch of a tree.
8. Fetch some sticks to lay the fire.
9. The box of nails weighs half a pound.
10. Men used to hunt animals with a spear.

LIST E

1. We read a fairy story after tea.
2. Father carried his white shirt upstairs.
3. The tits built a nest in the apple tree.
4. The boy likes bread and jam for tea.
5. Trees do not grow on high mountains.
6. Farmers usually cut their hay in June.
7. Put the glass jar under the water.
8. Don't come home without your cap.
9. Six o'clock is too late to start.
10. Very early houses had roofs of straw

Index

DATE DUE

APR 18 77			
NOV 11 76			
APR 07 77			
APR 14 77			
MAY 19 '77			
JAN 10 1980			
DEC 1 1 1986			
NOV 22 1988			
MAR 15 1993			
DEC 1 5 1996			
OCT 2 1 2002			
APR 1 6 2004			

HIGHSMITH 45-220   PRINTED IN U.S.A.